THE NATIONAL BOTANIC
GARDEN OF WALES

MESOZOIC

Time of the dinosaur.
First paw-print, first hoof-beat,
first mammals of swamp and shore,
first of the cold-bloods dreaming on stones.

And at its humid, balmy close,
ammonite and dinosaur dead,
rich silts flood the valleys,
and the garden begins.

THE NATIONAL BOTANIC GARDEN OF WALES

EDITED BY ANDREW SCLATER

WITH POEMS BY GILLIAN CLARKE

HarperCollins*Illustrated*

To all who helped in getting the
project started, and above all to
William Wilkins

First published in 2000 by HarperCollins*Illustrated*
an imprint of HarperCollins*Publishers*
77-85 Fulham Palace Road
London W6 8JB

The HarperCollins website address is:
www.**fireandwater**.com

Mapping on page 5 © Bartholomew Mapping Services

Extracts from Andrew Marvell's 'The Garden' taken
from *The Penguin Book of Renaissance Verse*, edited by H R
Woudhuysen (New York, 1993)

A CIP catalogue record for this book is available
from the British Library.

ISBN: 0 00 414091 5

Layout Design: Caroline Hill
Index: Chris Howes

04 02 00 01 03
2 4 6 8 9 7 5 3 1

Colour reproduction by Colourscan
Printed and bound in the UK by Bath Press
Colourbooks Ltd

ACKNOWLEDGEMENTS

So many people have contributed to the creation of the National Botanic Garden
of Wales. Too numerous to list, they all deserve our thanks. We should be
grateful too to the various organisations and companies who supported the
project as it gained momentum. Above all, the National Botanic Garden of Wales
is due to the tireless efforts of William Wilkins over nearly a decade.

For their part in the early days of the project, the editor wishes to thank David
Bown, Gerard Dent, Quentin Kay, Susan Lloyd-Fern, Thomas Lloyd, Barry
Long, Michael Maunder, Michael Norman, R Rockingham Gill, John Savidge
and others who contributed to the work of the first Steering Group. He also
wishes to remember the generous hospitality extended by Alison and Simon
Mostyn and Gilda and Jac Roberts.

The editor is particularly grateful to all the members of the Arts and Identity
Advisory Group, many of whom have written for this book. He also wishes to
thank Dan Clayton-Jones, Charles Stirton and William Wilkins for information
during the writing of 'Early Days of the Garden', and Willem Kuiters for
historical information on William Paxton.

At Foster and Partners the following people made an invaluable contribution:
Spencer de Grey, Nigel Curry, Katy Harris, David Jenkins, Gerard Forde, Nigel
Young and Elizabeth Walker.

John O'Neill and Alan Holland wish to thank David Littlewood, Chris Crowder
and Andrew Sclater for conversations and comments on their chapter. Michael
Rustin, who first mooted the idea of this book, wrote his chapter in memory of
Rachel Fruchter and her father Jan Gillett, botanist.

Finally, the editor could never have met the tight deadlines and high standards
required without the immeasurable support of his wife Shelley and, at
HarperCollins, of Victoria Alers-Hankey, Jacquie Brown, Polly Powell, and last
(but certainly not least) Fiona Screen. Very special thanks to them all.

The Garden would like to thank David Baird of the Millennium Commission, Dr
Quentin Kay, Dr John Savidge, Professor Dianne Edwards, and the Chairs of the
Advisory Groups – John Ellis, Fiona Peel and Charles Smart.

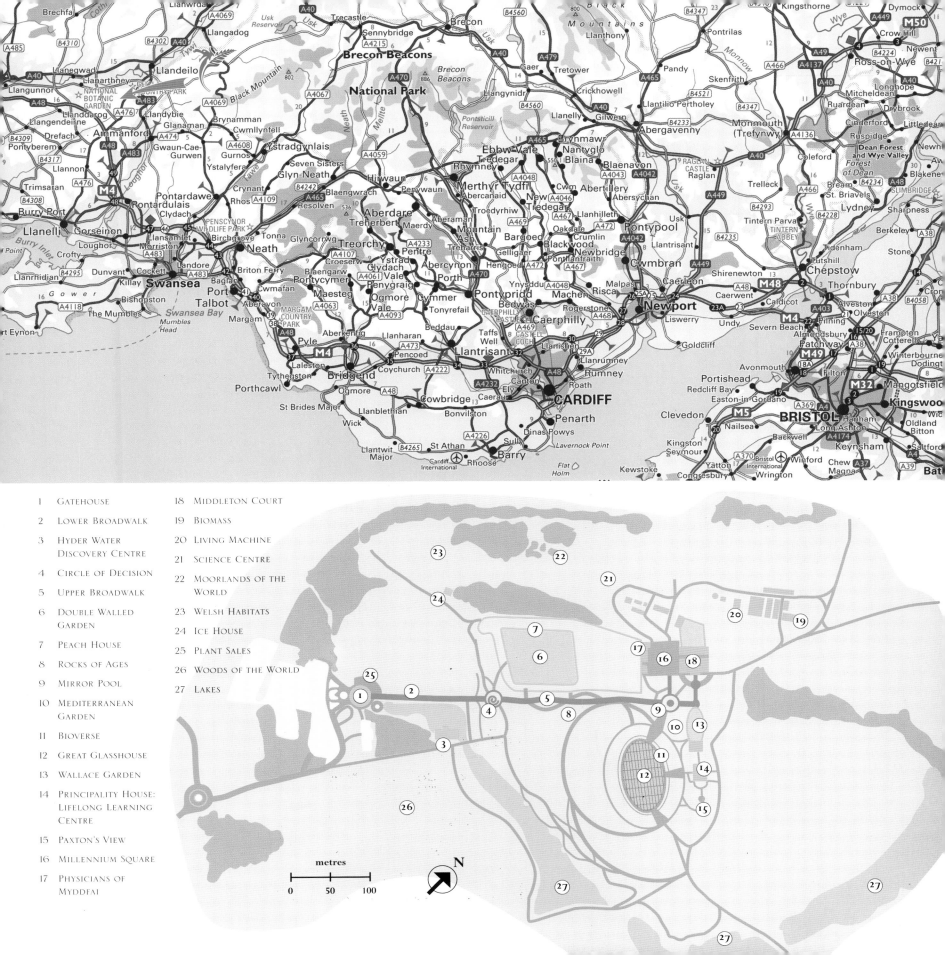

1   GATEHOUSE

2   LOWER BROADWALK

3   HYDER WATER
     DISCOVERY CENTRE

4   CIRCLE OF DECISION

5   UPPER BROADWALK

6   DOUBLE WALLED
     GARDEN

7   PEACH HOUSE

8   ROCKS OF AGES

9   MIRROR POOL

10 MEDITERRANEAN
     GARDEN

11 BIOVERSE

12 GREAT GLASSHOUSE

13 WALLACE GARDEN

14 PRINCIPALITY HOUSE:
     LIFELONG LEARNING
     CENTRE

15 PAXTON'S VIEW

16 MILLENNIUM SQUARE

17 PHYSICIANS OF
     MYDDFAI

18 MIDDLETON COURT

19 BIOMASS

20 LIVING MACHINE

21 SCIENCE CENTRE

22 MOORLANDS OF THE
     WORLD

23 WELSH HABITATS

24 ICE HOUSE

25 PLANT SALES

26 WOODS OF THE WORLD

27 LAKES

metres

0   50   100

N

CONTENTS

THE AUTHORS

Jan Morris is the author of *The Matter of Wales* (Oxford University Press, 1984, revised as *Wales*, Viking, 1998) and, in collaboration with her son, the Welsh-language poet Twm Morys, of *A Machynlleth Triad* (Viking, 1994). She is an Hon D Litt of the University of Wales.

Andrew Sclater was involved from the outset with the National Botanic Garden of Wales and chaired its first Steering Group, its Botanical, Horticultural and Environmental Sub-Committee and, latterly, the Arts and Identity Advisory Group. He runs his own landscape and garden consultancy, and has lectured and published widely on horticulture, garden history and aesthetics, both in the UK and abroad.

John Prest is an emeritus fellow of Balliol College, Oxford. He has written *The Garden of Eden: the Botanic Garden and the Re-creation of Paradise* (Yale University Press, 1981) and edited *The Illustrated History of Oxford University* (Oxford University Press, 1993).

Ivor Stokes trained at Kew. He was Curator of the City of Swansea's botanical collections before joining the National Botanic Garden of Wales as its Director of Horticulture.

Jay Appleton, Hon D Litt, is Emeritus Professor of Geography at Hull University. In *The Experience of Landscape* (Wiley, 1975, revised 1996), he advanced his Prospect-Refuge Theory of landscape aesthetics.

James Robertson is the author of a best-selling book on bats and a regular contributor to wildlife magazines. He is passionate about plants and is author/editor at the Countryside Council for Wales.

Lord Foster of Thames Bank established his architectural practice in 1967, and has received the Gold Medals of the Royal Institute of British Architects and the American Institute of Architects. In 1999 he received the Pritzker Architecture Prize. In 1997 the Queen appointed him to the Order of Merit and in 1999 he was made a Baron.

Peter Culley is an architect practising in London. He is project architect for the landscape in the Great Glasshouse and is currently working on the Crystal Palace Park scheme for John Lyall Architects and Gustafson Porter.

Hal Moggridge is principal of Colvin and Moggridge, the oldest landscape practice in Britain. He is a panellist for the National Trust, and a former President of the Landscape Institute, Royal Fine Arts Commissioner, Professor at the University of Sheffield, and Chairman of the Landscape Foundation.

Charles Stirton is Director of the National Botanic Garden of Wales. He is author of 106 scientific papers and editor of 4 books including *Advances in Legume Biology* (Missouri Botanical Garden, 1989) and *Weeds in a Changing World* (BCPC, 1995).

Rhodri Griffiths is the Science Development Officer at the National Botanic Garden of Wales. He recently completed a PhD in plant biochemistry and is interested in the chemistry of Welsh plants.

Peter Harper is Head of Biology at the Centre for Alternative Technology. He is the author of many books on green themes including *Radical Technology* (1976), *The Natural Garden Book* (1994), *Crazy Idealists!* (1995) and *Lifting the Lid* (1999). He is considered to be completely obsessed by compost.

Michael Rustin is a Professor of Sociology at the University of East London. He has previously published articles on cities and urban space, but never previously on gardens. He is co-editor of the magazine *Soundings*.

Kate Soper is Professor of Philosophy at the University of North London. She has published widely on ecological issues and worked as a journalist and translator. Her books include *Troubled Pleasures: Writings on Politics, Gender and Hedonism* (Verso, 1990) and *What is Nature?* (Blackwell, 1995).

John O'Neill is Professor of Philosophy at Lancaster University. His publications include *The Market: Ethics, Knowledge and Politics* (Routledge, 1998) and *Ecology, Policy and Politics: Human Well-Being and the Natural World* (Routledge, 1993), as well as numerous papers on environmental ethics, politics and economics.

Alan Holland is Professor of Applied Philosophy at Lancaster University and editor of the interdisciplinary journal *Environmental Values*. His recent work has focused on environmental decision-making and the analysis of certain policy objectives such as sustainability and ecological integrity.

Gilles Clément received the Grand Prix du Paysage in 1998 and is a gardener. His recent work includes the Parc André Citroën and Jardins de l'Arche (Paris), a garden at the Château de Blois and landscape designs for the Domaine de Rayol. He is the author of *Le Jardin en Mouvement* (Sens & Tonka, 1994) and *La Dernière Pierre* (Albin Michel, 1999).

Gillian Clarke is a poet. Recent collections include *Five Fields* (Carcanet, 1998) and *Nine Green Gardens* (Gomer, 2000). She lives on an 18-acre smallholding in Ceredigion.

ST. JAMES'S PALACE

Having followed the fortunes of the National Botanic Garden of Wales for rather more than a decade, I am pleased that this definitive book about the Garden is to be published. The guiding principles of the Garden - sustainability, conservation and education - are all things that matter to me, personally, and I was delighted to be invited to serve as Patron.

It is certainly exciting to think that Wales will soon have its own Botanic Garden, but I particularly welcome the way that this is to be achieved. Bringing this magnificent parkland landscape, with its necklace of lakes and Georgian buildings, back to life will be an admirable achievement in itself. The sensitive addition of new features will ensure that the whole Garden is worthy of its new title.

I am much looking forward to seeing the Garden in its opening year and am sure I shall be among a large number of people taking pride in the fact that Wales - at last - has such a splendid National Botanic Garden of its own.

O R I

G I N S

GARDEN OF WALES

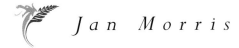

Jan Morris

A new century, a new Wales! This small country on the western flank of Europe already has its national assembly, its national university, its national library, its national museum and its national opera, not to mention its national rugby team. It is especially proper that at this moment of hope and renewal it should also have its National Botanic Garden, for there are few peoples that have been more intimately involved with the soil beneath their feet than the Welsh – traditionally a nation above all of farmers and miners.

There used to be times when despairing Welsh patriots, condemned it seemed to perpetual national humiliation, felt that the land itself was all they could truly call their own. It is not surprising that down the ages the Welsh mind has been preoccupied with idioms of nature. Through dappled woodland glades the ancient story-tellers take us, through thickets and dark forests, and nature itself is seen as an amalgam of the magical and the earthy. The greatest of medieval Welsh poets, Dafydd ap Gwilym, imagined a nightingale raising the sacred Host in a grove of green hazels: for like many another mystic, like many a Welsh herbalist and healer too, he saw all Wales as the Garden of God.

Isolated for so many centuries in this remote and demanding country, over the ages the Welsh farmer was intensely involved in the natural world, the source of his living, his health, his myths and his superstitions: and in those parts of the country where industry fell, it was mostly industry of an elemental kind – not the making of things, or the putting together of things, but the extraction of matter out of the earth itself. The coal dust of the pit was not so different from the mud of the farm.

Nevertheless when we think of Wales we do not habitually think of gardens. There are splendid show gardens in this country of

course – think of Bodnant, think of Powis Castle – and countless Welsh householders are proud of their flowerbeds or window boxes. In general, though, I think it fair to say that gardens and Welshness do not generally go together. The Welsh cottage of dreams is not bowered in honeysuckle, as ideal English cottages are, nor climbed about by roses and wisteria. It is a more austere kind of paradise, solid, tough, self-sufficient, and all too often deposited so romantically on a mountain slope, or on the edge of a peat bog, that it is no place for phlox or wallflower. Mosses and ferns, small wild daffodils, wood anemones and yellow poppies – these are the true domestic plants of Wales, and it is no coincidence that the national plant is not a flower at all, but a kind of onion.

In Wales, too, there was never the plethora of big country houses that has bequeathed to England such a treasury of fine gardens. The indigenous gentry was a working gentry of farming and sporting squires: literature often engaged their leisure hours, but seldom I think the making of gardens, although it was a Welsh gentleman, the great Oxford botanist and antiquarian Edward Llwyd, who first identified *Lloydia serotina*, Snowdon Lily, the rarest of Welsh alpine plants. Anyway, Wales came to be considered pre-eminently the country of the Picturesque, an aesthetic concept that was more concerned with the wild and the ruined than with the cultivated. Valentine Morris of Piercefield, near Chepstow, made his famous gardens part of the Wye valley itself, with glades, cliff paths and dells above the river; and when Thomas Johnes built himself a veritable Xanadu of the Picturesque, Hafod Uchtryd near Cwmystwyth, the gardens he created were as close as could be to the organic order of things – nature exploited perhaps, or even improved, but never challenged.

Critics used to postulate, indeed, that the Welsh as people had no sense of visual beauty. A large proportion of them lived in a countryside, by and large, of greys and greens and blacks – slate greys, mountain greens, coal blacks – which is why, so it used to be said, they had produced a prodigious number of writers, but few painters. The theory is discredited now, but it is true I think that many of the most gifted Welsh people have not much cared how their immediate surroundings looked. There was beauty enough in nature beyond the front gate, and in the design of their houses they were generally concerned to make a building seem

OPPOSITE *The Garden's local landscape: the Tywi Valley seen from Paxton's Tower, built in 1815 as an eyecatcher in the Park at Middleton Hall.*

GYFERBYN *Y tirlun lleol: golwg dros Ddyffryn Tywi o Dŵr Paxton a godwyd o ran gorchest ym 1815 yn Neuadd Middleton.*

simply part of the landscape – as the Welsh-descended Frank Lloyd Wright put it, not to be on the hill, but of it. When I myself contemplated the reorganisation of my small garden in Gwynedd, I found myself obeying some immemorial ancestral instinct of my own, and wanting it to be like the bottom of a wood.

Of course this does not mean that the Welsh are aloof to the wonders and needs of the natural environment. How could they be, living in a country that still so often seems, even now, so allegorically close to the Creation? Any stranger in Wales must be struck by its profligacy of nature – lush pastures beside harsh moorlands, sheep wherever you look, Constable cattle grazing water meadows, forests mysterious and depressingly prosaic, kites and buzzards and ravens and choughs, the sea on three sides, the great bare mountains all down the middle. And basic to it all the variety of the botanical life, from the corn to the dandelion, the heather and the gorse to the feral rhododendron, which clothes so much of our little country in its living mantle.

So it is right that in one of the most fecund parts of all Wales, along the river valley where the poet John Dyer, a couple of hundred years ago, wrote his great panegyric to nature in Wales – that in the heart of the Tywi Valley the latest and perhaps the loveliest of our national institutions should be established, to celebrate the marvels of botanical life all over the world, and not least in Wales itself. Dyer wrote of his Grongar Hill that

> *Grass and flowers Quiet treads,*
> *On the meads and mountain-heads,*
> *Along with Pleasure, close ally'd,*
> *Ever by each other's side.*

The National Botanic Garden will be the greatest of Welsh pleasure gardens, but it will have profound scientific and educational purposes too: and above all it will be a sort of pledge of Welsh allegiance – beyond pleasure or politics, beyond crass materialism or even science – to Nature itself.

GARDD CYMRU

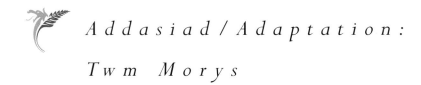

Addasiad/Adaptation:

Twm Morys

Canrif newydd, Cymru newydd! Mae gynnon ni Gynulliad Cenedlaethol, a Phrifysgol Genedlaethol, a Llyfrgell Genedlaethol, ac Amgueddfa Genedlaethol, a Chwmni Opera Cenedlaethol, a thîm Rygbi Cenedlaethol. A dyma ni, yn briodol iawn ar ryw adeg o egino mawr fel hyn, am gael Gardd Genedlaethol hefyd! Ychydig iawn o genhedloedd fu cymaint ynghlwm â'r pridd, ar y tir ac odano fo â'r Cymry.

Mi fu adegau tywyll, a'r wlad fel petai hi am fod o dan yr iau am dragwyddoldeb, pan oedd rhai yng Nghymru'n teimlo mai'r tir oedd yr unig beth oedd piau nhw yn iawn. Pa ryfedd fod llond pen y Cymro drwy'r canrifoedd o ddelweddau natur? Drwy'r llannerch a'r llwyni yr â'r hen gyfarwyddiaid â ni, a lledrith a phridd yn gymysg ydi natur yn eu chwedlau nhw. A dyna ichi Dafydd ap Gwilym yn gweld yr eos yn codi'r afrlladen 'hyd y nen uwchben y berth.' Yr un fath ag i lawer dyn hysbys a meddyg llysiau, gardd Duw oedd Cymru i gyd iddo fo.

Bu'r ffarmwr o Gymro yng nghanol natur drwy'r oesoedd. Dyna ffynhonnell ei fywoliaeth, ei iechyd, ei chwedlau a'i ofergoelion. Ac yn y mannau hynny lle cododd diwydiant, rhyw ddiwydiant go elfennol oedd hwnnw. Nid gwneud pethau, neu roi pethau at ei gilydd, ond tynnu deunydd o'r ddaear ei hun. Doedd llwch y pwll ddim yn annhebig iawn i fwd y ffarm, a gweithio'r pridd roedd y glowr a'r ffarmwr fel ei gilydd.

Ond nid am erddi y byddwn ni'n meddwl, rywsut, wrth feddwl am Gymru. Mae 'na erddi gwych iawn, wrth reswm, fel gardd Bodnant a gardd Castell Powys. Ac mae llond gwlad o arddwyr bychain balch. Ond efallai nad ydi gerddi a Chymreigrwydd yn cyd-fynd yn rhyw hwylus iawn. Does dim gwyddfid yn sbloets dros y bwthyn Cymreig delfrydol, fel sydd dros fythynod del y Sais, na rhosod na wistaria. Paradwys fwy gerwin ydi hon, yn gadarn a gwydn a hunan-gynhaliol. Ac yn amlach na heb wedi ei sodro ar allt serth, neu wrth ymyl rhyw fawnog, lle na fydd y ladi fach wen na'r jinifflwar yn mentro byth. Mwsog a rhedyn, a chennin Pedr bach gwyllt, blodau'r gwynt a phabis melyn – dyna ichi blanhigion Cymru yn iawn. Ac nid cyd-ddigwyddiad ydi nad blodyn mo'n planhigyn cenedlaethol ni, ond math o nionyn.

Doedd gan y Cymry chwaith mo'r cannoedd o blastai sy wedi rhoi i Loegr y fath gyfoeth o erddi godidog. Byddigions oedd yn ffarmio ac yn hela oedd ein byddigions ni. Cerddi, nid gerddi, oedd diléit eu horiau hamdden. A phrun bynnag, fel Gwlad y Pictwrèsg y daethpwyd i feddwl am Gymru yn benna', nes bod mwy o fri ar dir anial ac adfeilion nag ar dir âr. Dyna erddi enwog Piercefield, tŷ Valentine Morris ger Cas-went, er enghraifft. Mi wnaed y rheini yn rhan o Ddyffryn Gwy, yn llanerchau, a llwybrau pennau gelltydd, a phantiau uwchlaw'r afon; a gerddi Hafod Uchtryd, y Xanadu o dŷ a gododd Thomas Johnes yng Nghwm Ystwyth, oedd mor agos ag yr oedd modd i drefn natur. Manteisio ar natur, a cheisio'i gwella hi, hwyrach, ond heb ei herio hi byth.

Mae 'na ryw duedd wedi bod i feddwl nad oedd gan y Cymry lygad i weld harddwch. Llwyd a gwyrdd a du oedd byd y rhelyw ohonyn nhw. Llwyd y llechi, gwyrdd y mynydd, du'r glo. A dyna pam, medden' nhw, fod faint fyd fynnir o lenorion Cymraeg, ond ychydig o arlunwyr. Mae llai o fynd bellach ar y ddamcaniaeth honno. Ond hwyrach ei bod hi'n wir na fu fawr o ots gan y Cymry mwya' disglair sut le i edrych arno fo oedd eu milltir sqwâr nhw. Roedd harddwch natur y tu draw i'r llidiart. Ac wrth godi tŷ, y nod yn y bôn oedd iddo fo edrych fel petai o wedi tyfu o'r tir. Nid ar y bryn, ond o'r bryn, chwedl Frank Lloyd Wright. Pan ddaeth hi'n bryd rhoi trefn ar y tipyn gardd acw yn Eifionydd, roedd rhyw hen reddf gyndeidiol yn mynnu ei bod hi'n cael ei gwneud yn debig i lawr y coed.

Dydi hynny ddim yn golygu, cofiwch, fod y Cymry yn ddihitio ynghylch rhyfeddodau ac anghenion yr amgylchfyd. Sut y gallen ni fod, a ninnau'n byw mewn gwlad sydd hyd heddiw mor alegoraidd agos i'r Cread ei hun? Syndod mawr i'r ymwelydd, yn siŵr ichi, ydi ei hamrywiaeth naturiol hi. Y porfeydd ir wrth ymyl

y ffriddoedd garw, y defaid ym mhob man, y gwartheg at eu fferau yn y dŵr, y coedwigoedd dirgel, a'r rhai unffurf diflas, y barcutiaid a'r boncathod a'r cigfrain a'r brain coesgoch, y môr ar dair ochr, y moelni maith drwy'r canol. A'r bywyd botanegol sy'n hanfod i'r cwbwl, yr ŷd a dant y llew, y grug a'r eithin, a'r rhododendron sy'n ei rhempio hi dros gymaint o'n gwlad fechan ni.

A phriodol iawn o beth hefyd ydi mai yn un o ardaloedd mwya' toreithiog Cymru, sef Dyffryn Tywi, y bydd ein sefydliad cenedlaethol diweddara' a hardda' ni, yn dathlu rhyfeddodau'r bywyd botanegol yng Nghymru, a thrwy'r byd i gyd. Yn Nyffryn Tywi lle mae'r 'gwyrthiau'n drwm dros ddôl a pherth a phren', chwedl James Eirian Davies. Yr Ardd Genedlaethol hon fydd y fwya' o Erddi Pleser Cymru. Ond bydd iddi hefyd amcanion gwyddonol ac addysgiadol. Ac yn anad dim, mi fydd hi fel rhyw lw o deyrngarwch – y tu hwnt i wleidyddiaeth a materoldeb a gwyddoniaeth – i Natur ei hun.

ABOVE *Llyn y fan fach, Carmarthenshire, from whose waters appeared the beautiful mother of the three Physicians of Myddfai.*

UCHOD *Llyn y fan fach yn Sir Gaerfyrddin. O ddyfroedd hwn y daeth mam hardd Meddygon enwog Myddfai.*

INTRODUCTION:
A GARDEN IS BORN

Andrew Sclater

OPPOSITE *Autumn-flowering* Echinacea purpurea *by Llyn Uchaf — beyond the water, the hillock that is to become the Woodlands of the World.*

RIGHT *View from The Broadwalk through a planting of yellow composites towards the Hyder Water Discovery Centre.*

A new garden is born! Observe it carefully — you will notice changes week after week, month after month and year after year, as you would in a child. The way that it develops will depend on the events and circumstances it encounters during its formative years. As the infant grows and responds to its personal encounters, its personality will emerge: the product of a time and a consciousness that is in sympathy with nature, as this book relates. Through its plant collections from different regions of the Earth, and through its environmental themes too, the garden may prompt us to reflect upon the place of humans in nature and it will offer some responses to our concerns. In this way, the garden is not only about the biological growth of plants, but it is also about the growth and development of our culture, incorporating many facets of our shared contemporary concerns for the environment.

This book is indeed about a garden of the future. In writing these pages, we have asked ourselves what it means to make a national botanic garden now, and both designers and staff have shared their thoughts about the first steps towards the future identity of the National Botanic Garden of Wales. In reading, and perhaps in visiting the garden, you too will have your thoughts. As water and nutrients are to the growth of plants, so ideas and reflection are to the growth of an endeavour such as this. It would be impossible to cover all possible ways of thinking about a botanic garden of the 21st century, so we have emphasised aspects which take botany beyond

the confines of science. It is a distinguishing feature of this new botanic garden that it is not only a scientific project. Art too will have its place, as the garden takes on new dimensions. Education is a keystone not only for children but also for adults in the Lifelong Learning Centre. Art, science and education will all be framed in relation to the needs of plants and the needs of people. Plants and people together is what the garden is for.

The National Botanic Garden of Wales occupies the former estate of Middleton Hall in Carmarthenshire, in the tract of land which separates the lush Tywi Valley from Dylan Thomas' beloved

coastline stretching from Mumbles Bay via the Gower peninsula to Llansteffan in South Wales. This is the garden's physical location, and the physical development of its main features is described in these pages, by the designers themselves. The other contributors consider the garden as a new element in a world of ideas and aspirations. We have asked ourselves what it means to create a new botanic garden now, and on a scale that far surpasses any such venture in Britain for many generations. The book allows you, the reader, to find this garden on the map of Wales, and on the map of Western culture too.

The book benefits from Gillian Clarke's beautiful poems, which illustrate the link between the Garden and Art. She conjures up many beautiful connections between humans and the natural world in the poems that she wrote especially for Middleton, and which you will find throughout the book. They set the whole endeavour of the botanic garden in a universal frame. She expands time beyond the long history of botanic gardens back into geological time, to the dinosaurs and coral reefs of Wales, inspired by the geological formations from which the boulders of the The Broadwalk were taken. But the car makes its appearance too in her verse *Taking the Planet Home*, reminding us that we are aware of a world of wilderness and elemental creation beyond the windscreen, among the stars. The car can indeed allow us to think of nature, if only by the contrast which it makes between the natures of human and other lives. There are stark contrasts in the natural world too.

SILURIAN

Ystrad Meurig. Aberystwyth grit
from stormy deposits in water too deep for life.

And just as old, the fossil shells
of Llandovery's shallow seas.

Gillian Clarke

El Niño in the Walled Garden reinforces the idea of the garden as a shelter for vulnerable species against the destructive force of the storm. The protection, love and nurture of plants require an attitude of mind that is sympathetic to our environment.

In 'Origins', our opening section, John Prest sets the scene by reminding us that, in the earliest days of botanic gardens, the discovery of new plants in far-off continents led to questions of a theological nature. The botanic garden represented a restored Eden where species that had sometime been dispersed from the original Eden between the Tigris and Euphrates rivers could at last be brought together again as in the days of Adam and Eve. Next, under the influence of the Renaissance and Humanism, the botanic garden took on the role of a place of learning in which plants, as natural phenomena, could be studied. Italy, seat of the Renaissance, had the first modern botanic gardens. Germany, the Netherlands, France, and Britain followed. These early gardens were often attached to universities, and the particular branch of knowledge that they served was medicine, or 'physic' as it was once known. Only one of Britain's botanic gardens still preserves the name – The Chelsea Physic Garden – founded in 1673 by the Society of Apothecaries. By the 18th century, the earlier discoveries of far-off lands had prompted European powers to establish colonies and to exploit them. During the entire period of European imperialism, the botanic gardens became testing

ABOVE *The Chelsea Physic Garden, the only British botanic garden to retain the link with medicine in its name.*

TOP LEFT *Scotland's national botanic garden at Edinburgh was founded in 1670 – 330 years before its Welsh counterpart!*

TOP RIGHT *This crocus-spangled glade at Kew exudes the confidence of empire and royal patronage.*

BELOW *The* Canna *in front of this glasshouse at Kew first came to Britain from the West Indies.*

grounds where the usefulness and economic value of the indigenous plants of the colonies could be assessed. The gardens participated in a drive to enrich the coloniser at the expense of the colonised.

But if the mission of earlier gardens was to exploit plants, whether for medicine or other profitable means, my story of the early days of the National Botanic Garden of Wales shifts the focus to a range of different concerns. First, a generalised concern for the environment now pervades Western culture. So, our new botanic garden has to contribute to conservation. And its mission includes a commitment to reflect the relationship between human beings and their environment. This relationship is not a simple one but takes many forms, one of which is the new cultural interest in plants exemplified, on the one hand, by Richard Mabey's recent best-seller *Flora Britannica* (1996), and on the other, by the founding principles of the National Botanic Garden of Wales or, indeed, its sister Millennium project, the Eden Project in Cornwall. While John Prest's history spans more than five centuries, my story of the genesis of the National Botanic Garden of Wales spans little more than a decade. But the garden is only just beginning, and the patronage of the Prince of Wales seems to indicate that it will grow to dignified maturity, like its 17th- and 18th-century counterparts at Edinburgh and Kew, both of which are royal gardens.

ABOVE *'Dereliction with snowdrops' – the Walled Garden before work began.*

RIGHT *A country lane close to the site of the National Botanic Garden.*

In 'Plants and Landscape' Ivor Stokes, Head of Horticulture, with responsibilty for the welfare of the plants at the National Botanic Garden, explains the Garden's approach to planting. The Garden's Woodlands of the World are not made up of isolated specimens, but reproduce whole communities including the tree canopy, shrubs and herbaceous plants that are to be found, for example, in Chinese or Chilean woods. A horticulture that is sympathetic to nature is exemplified by the moorland communities from other countries planted on the old red sandstone hill west of the Walled Garden, and by the re-creation of prairies and steppes. At the core of all this work is an attempt to mirror, in the Garden, the conditions which different plant communities experience in their natural habitats. We cannot deny that the making of a garden is an unnatural act, but the Head of Horticulture is doing the gardening as naturally as possible. And if the Great Glasshouse is triumphantly unnatural, its internal environment is designed to meet the needs of species from the various mediterranean climatic zones. In all of this, human ingenuity demonstrates its adaptation to, and sympathy for, nature.

There is something entirely novel about one of the foremost British botanic gardens being sited in the countryside. Edinburgh

and Kew are in capital cities, but Cardiff to Middleton is some 65 miles. Is this a disadvantage? Certainly, city folk would rather have it closer. But the remote setting also reflects a change in our attitude to nature since the earlier gardens were founded. First, it seems more proper now to accommodate nature's plants in an environment that is more natural than the city. Secondly, local character and local communities are gaining more recognition than formerly, and the gap between city and country is narrowing. In my chapter The 'Genius' and Histories of Middleton, I take you around the Middleton countryside with one eye on its natural history and one eye looking back to another history – that of some of the people who contributed in the past to making Middleton the great estate we see today. Visitors will be struck by the landscape beauty and clean green qualities of Middleton. The site matches Raymond Williams' description of his birthplace in 'remote . . . very old settled countryside' and 'a few miles beyond it the first industrial towns and villages of the great coal and steel area of South Wales'. Williams came from the east of that great area and Middleton lies to the west, in the unspoilt countryside beyond the 'industrial fringe'. The car that takes us to Middleton contrasts

starkly with the respect for nature of which I have spoken, but in bringing us to the countryside, to Middleton, it brings us into nature in another sense. There are lessons to be learned from contemplating the differences between the natural environment and the networks of human constructions that run through it.

Jay Appleton asks 'what is the Welsh landscape?'. The National Botanic Garden needs to understand the answers to that question if it is to gain an idea of the messages it will convey simply by being where it is. The portrayal of Wales in literature, and its place in the history of what is considered as 'picturesque', both contribute to the ways in which we appreciate its landscape. Jay Appleton uses the model of the botanic garden in Canberra, New South Wales, to show how a created place can make direct connections with the landscape beyond it. In Canberra's case, the surroundings are native eucalyptus forest within which the garden exists as an island. So it naturally becomes part of a landscape that is original to its land. Its forest setting is not the only physical symbol of the character of Australia, since some of Canberra's great monuments are visible from the garden too. Although Middleton has no native forest to set it off, it is surrounded by the small fields and hedgerows of unspoilt

BELOW Sheep and the ancient oak typify the landscape of Carmarthenshire.

countryside that typify its local landscape and associate it closely with the history of life on the land of Wales.

James Robertson pursues the theme of plants by showing the degree to which, for centuries, human beings in Wales have developed special relationships with their vegetation. He gives a fascinating account of medicinal, agricultural, industrial and many other uses of plants, specific to Wales. He tells the story of Welsh botany from the 16th century to the present, and relates the climate and geology of Wales to its native flora. As more than two-thirds of all species in Britain grow in Wales, it is clear why a national botanic garden had to be created. It is clear, too, that there is a need for greater effort to be devoted to conservation. The chapter draws to a disturbing close with statistics on the shrinking areas of certain natural habitats in Wales, and on the outright loss of scores of species from the Welsh countryside. Botanists in the Garden will rise to the challenge of understanding these trends in the hope that they are reversible.

In 'Design', Norman Foster, Peter Culley and Hal Moggridge together describe the designs which have given the old estate its breathtaking new structures and garden layout. The Great Glasshouse is shown by Norman Foster to belong to a utilitarian type of building which has influenced architectural history by bringing new engineering and structural techniques to the attention of architects. He sees the glasshouse as no less than the midwife of modern architecture. Peter Culley's account of Gustafson Porter's work includes exciting drawings and sketches that reveal the daring simplicity of Kathryn Gustafson's idea for adding internal height to the Great Glasshouse by creating a rock-lined ravine. The naturalistic irregularity of its interior contrasts with the clean, spare lines of the Glasshouse superstructure. The effectiveness of this contrast draws its strength from the way that it embodies the two poles of the garden's essence: 'nature' and 'artifice'. Hal Moggridge tells the story of the process which brought the landscape design into being. We learn from him that it was no simple task to re-organise an existing design to incorporate new elements.

Together these designers have written a new chapter onto Middleton's landscape and have added new dimensions to the Garden's journey into the future.

ABOVE *Primeval,*
postmodern and Ark-like,
the Great Glasshouse
has come to rest on a
green hill.

In 'Science & Society', the Botanic Garden's Director, Charles Stirton, and Science Development Officer, Rhodri Griffiths, show that science in a new botanic garden must incorporate ethics and social responsibility. It may come as something of a surprise that the work of classifying plants, begun by Theophrastus and organised, in the 18th century, by Linnaeus into the basic form used today, still needs refining. Traditionally, this is the central role of the botanic garden but one that must keep up with advances in science. Their chapter also recognises that questions will be asked of science's direction and purposes. Current issues surrounding genetic modification of plants are explored impartially within the National Botanic Garden of Wales so as to allow visitors the better to consider their position.

Most in Western society now believe that environmental awareness is crucial to the future of the planet. Peter Harper questions certain basic assumptions about the right way of increasing this awareness. Sometimes, popular ideas and principles may not actually be the best way forward. It is sobering to think that after thirty years of popular ecology, we still have so much to understand and resolve. While the chapter offers no simple solutions, it does testify to the need for better understanding. The National Botanic Garden provides a structure in which to refine and improve environmental practices and demonstrate these to a large number of people.

The notion of ecosystem is a product of the science of ecology and applies to biological systems, but Michael Rustin, a sociologist, reconsiders this idea as a means of understanding society itself. In so doing, he reduces the apparent distance between humans and nature. It is exciting to think that frames of reference used by biologists to understand ways in which organisms interrelate may throw light on social processes too.

In 'Nature and Future', Kate Soper, John O'Neill and Alan Holland further examine what 'nature' itself means, and the extent to which humans are part of, or apart from, it. Their contributions demonstrate convincingly that there is no easy way of knowing exactly what 'nature' is, nor of knowing exactly how we should act as its custodians or managers. As society changes, so does the idea of nature, as do the governing principles of conservation practice. The planet is changing and humans are contributing to that change. But human activities are almost certainly not the only causes of global change. In Gilles Clément's chapter, we learn that plants are moving across the Earth in surprising ways. His views challenge the idea that scarcity is what we should value and protect. Some plants are aggressive conquerors which seemingly displace weaker species. Although humans may assist these processes, losses in certain species are compensated for by the increased successes and abundance of others. Should this cause us to reconsider our attitudes towards conservation? For Gilles Clément, the answer may lie in a better understanding of the ways in which plants move across the Earth and he proposes that the classification of plants should be revised to take account of their behaviour rather than focussing only on the characteristics of their structures and components, as hitherto.

The book ends with these philosophical questions. They demonstrate that modern science has not answered all of the great questions and that we are still unsettled in the ways in which we relate to nature. The exciting ground which the book covers pays little heed to the old boundaries between science and art, and between science and society. In raising the possibility of a humanist botanic garden, Gilles Clément prompts us to consider a revision of the way that a botanic garden frames its purpose. Now that the good of humanity seems to be inextricably bound up with preservation of the whole planet and its biology, there is a case to be made for expanding horizons in the way that we think about the National Botanic Garden of Wales.

The National Botanic Garden's Arts and Identity Advisory Group has provided many of the book's contributors. The Garden's staff nicknamed us 'the philosophers' – a double-edged compliment which certainly distanced us from the massive practical difficulties which daily faced the 'doers' involved in the massive building programme. But, cast in the role of philosophers, we were able to consider the meaning of gardens in general, and more particularly the paths which lead from different aspects of contemporary culture towards the idea of a National Botanic Garden of Wales.

Indeed, history honours the garden as a proper place for reflection. Both ancient Greeks and Druids planted sacred groves around their temples. In Athens and other major Greek towns, trees provided the shade needed for discussion and philosophy. Plato, Aristotle and Epicurus, pre-Christian thinkers whose works underpin much of Western thought even to this day, all developed their theories in the open air of public gardens. Of greatest interest to botanists was Theophrastus (c. 370–286 BC) whose philosophical works included classification of human characters and faults, and extended to plants too. His *Enquiry into Plants* was the first systematic description of all known species, establishing him as the father of botany and perhaps his garden may have been the first botanic garden on Earth.

Science and philosophy are, therefore, ancient and honourable elements of a garden. In the Christian tradition, Genesis places the Tree of Knowledge at the centre of the Garden of Eden. Connections like this allow us to shift between physical gardens and metaphysics. Eden connects to Paradise, and thus that garden was the perfect place. The origin of our word 'paradise' derives from the Greek writer Xenophon (c. 430–354 BC), who used the term *paradeisos* to signify royal gardens containing fruit, ornamental trees, flowers, birds and animals (but apparently no humans!) in a vast enclosure. *Paradeisos*, in turn, derived from the even earlier Islamic word *pairidaêza* for an enclosure or park. Our word means heaven, and our notion of heaven is set in the tradition of gardens and parks. Thus gardens are symbols of heaven and perfection, and not only in Christian thought. In Islamic literature, too, the garden is often invoked to symbolise life, love and the human soul.

Leaving the garden of the spirit for our botanic garden, in which gardening, art and science are united, we could not do better than leave the last word to Dylan Thomas, who was born and brought up so close to Middleton:

The force that through the green fuse drives the flower
Drives my green age; that blasts the roots of trees
Is my destroyer.
And I am dumb to tell the crooked rose
My youth is bent by the same wintry fever.

If the ancients favoured gardens for philosophy, then gardens are inextricably linked to the love, study, and pursuit of wisdom, and to the use of knowledge in the understanding of things and their causes. The National Botanic Garden of Wales has started out with the pursuit of knowledge at its core. Building on earlier knowledge from a wide range of sources, opening new horizons in the traditions established by the older botanic gardens, bringing together science and art, acknowledging the physical and metaphysical in nature, the National Botanic Garden of Wales adds a new dimension to the future of botany. For as a garden, it can trace close and ancient links to so much that is important in human culture.

LEFT *The Boat House at Laugharne – Dylan Thomas's home from 1949 until his death in 1953.*

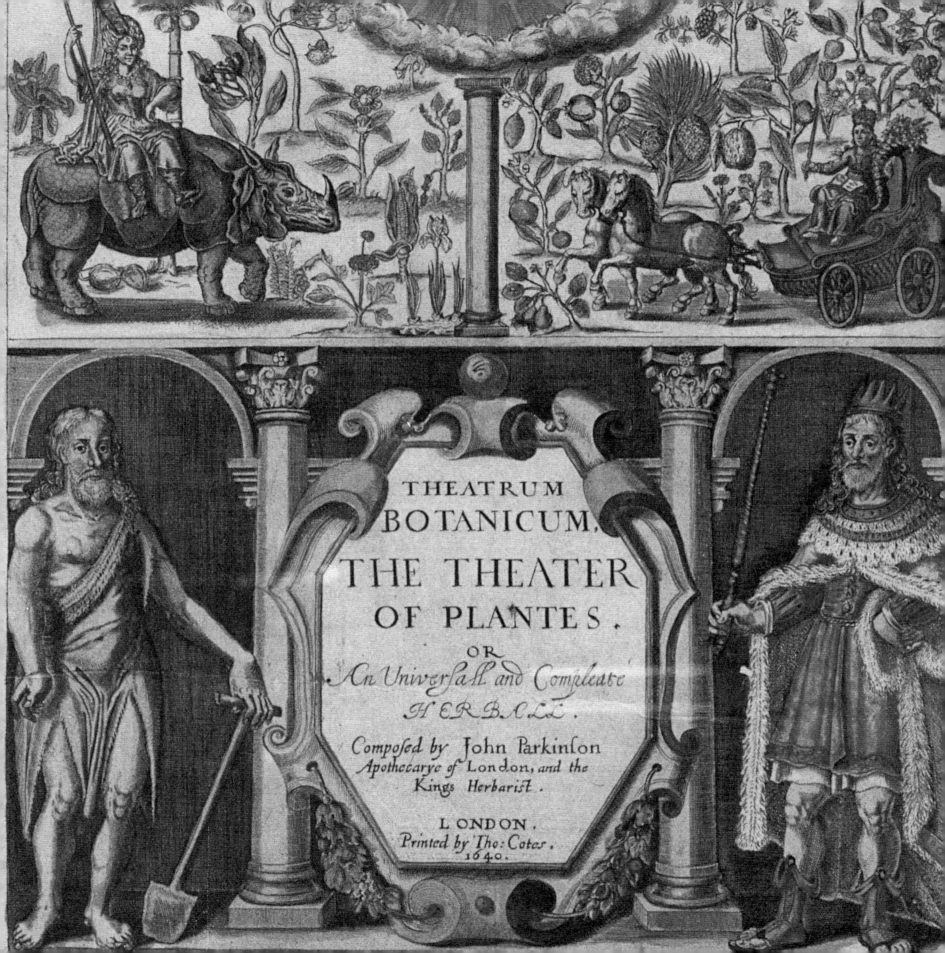

THEATRUM
BOTANICUM,
THE THEATER
OF PLANTES.
OR
An Universall and Compleate
HERBALL.

Composed by John Parkinson
Apothecarye of London, and the
Kings Herbarist.

LONDON.
Printed by Tho: Cotes.
1640.

THE HISTORY OF BOTANIC GARDENS

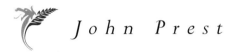

John Prest

Collections of plants were valued by ancient Greek philosophers, Chinese emperors, Persian princes, Arab doctors, medieval monks and nuns, and by Montezuma in Mexico City. But the history of the modern botanic garden begins with the invention, by the Portuguese, of the ocean-going ship in the 15th century and the European discovery of America and a new biota. Since that time there have been two kinds of botanic garden, the university botanic garden and the applied botanic garden.

THE UNIVERSITY BOTANIC GARDEN
In the 16th century Christian theologians asked how the hitherto unknown peoples, animals and plants fitted into the story of the origins of the world as told in Genesis. God had placed all the plants and animals in the original Garden and invited Adam to name them. When had the American ones become separated from the remainder? Was it as a consequence of the Fall or the Flood? Whatever the answer, it was now possible to gather the scattered pieces of the creation together from the four corners of the earth, Europe, Asia, Africa and America, and reunite them in a new Garden of Eden. The more exotic species the garden contained, the more it would tell the philosopher about the nature of the Creator. Sheltered by walls, and warmed by stoves and flues, the climate in such a garden might approximate to the 'perpetual spring' in which the first trees had flowered and borne fruit

continuously, and Adam and Eve had lived without labour, in innocence of their nakedness.

The re-creation of paradise was prominent among the motives for the foundation of botanic gardens at Pisa (1543), Padua (1545), Bologna (1567), Leipzig (1579), Leyden (1587) and Montpellier (1593) in the 16th century, and at Oxford (1621), Paris (1626), and other places in the 17th century. These were all university towns and every one of these botanic gardens became the workplace for a professor of botany and a professor of medicine.

There could be no botanical science without a standard system of plant names. The first task of a professor in a university garden, then, was to classify plants into families and, like Adam before him, to name them. New arrivals poured in from the East as well as from the West, and the Montpelliérains, especially, won renown for their contribution to the study of taxonomy. The number of known species increased rapidly from the 6,000 described by Bauhin at the beginning of the 17th century to the 80,000 known to William Hooker when he was professor of botany at the University of Glasgow in 1825. Between these two dates the works produced by the great botanists, John Ray of Cambridge, Carl Linné (Linnaeus) in Uppsala, and Pitton de Tournefort, de Jussieu and Alphonse de Candolle at Paris, reveal their concern with system, order and scientific principles.

OPPOSITE *John Parkinson's frontispiece featured Adam, Solomon and the four continents, Asia and Europe (above), and Africa and America (not shown here).*

God had appointed the green herb for medicine, and many botanists were physicians. But physic, like taxonomy, advanced slowly. The preparation of simples was an inexact science, and case-notes about patients and the supposed reasons for their recovery or decline were unreliable and difficult to compare. Not all plants possessed healing 'virtues'. Many were poisonous, though some of these, like the foxglove, might be administered in small doses. Rhubarb was injurious in one part and beneficial in another. But new-world plants might yield cures for old-world injuries and diseases. Monardes praised, and Clusius popularised, the American plants which were reaching Seville in the 16th century. Nineteenth-century medical botanies reveal how, over the long run, the pharmacopoeia was enlarged. In addition to time-honoured local remedies like sorrel for cooling fevers, elder for stimulation, valerian for sedation, henbane for narcosis and so on, there were expensive medicines like asafoetida from Iran, ipecacuanha from Brazil, and sarsaparilla from North America. Those suffering from chronic catarrh, dysentery, and syphilis were grateful for them.

ABOVE *In the days before pacemakers, foxglove* (Digitalis) *could be used to regulate the heartbeat.*

LEFT *Andreini (1617) pictured Adam standing just outside the Garden of Eden to name the animals. It has never been easy to combine botanical gardens and zoological gardens.*

acclimatisation in their settlements at the Cape of Good Hope, Ceylon and Java. In 1706 a single celebrated coffee plant reached the botanic garden in Amsterdam. Its seeds were sent to Surinam, whence they were smuggled to Brazil, and also to Paris, and from Paris to Martinique. The realisation that plants which flourished in the tropical East Indies might grow in the Caribbean took hold of the European imagination. The West Indian islands lay at less than half the distance of the spice islands, and were, following the extinction of the indigenous inhabitants by European diseases (smallpox and measles), much easier to control.

In the 18th century the French set up a formal botanical establishment centred on the *Jardin du Roi* at Paris, with dependent gardens in Mauritius and La Réunion in the Indian Ocean, and in Martinique, Guadeloupe and Dominica in the West Indies. Pierre Poivre seized pepper plants, and cinnamon, nutmeg and clove trees from the Dutch-held coasts of Indonesia, and transferred them from one side of the world to the other. One garden selected the varieties to be sent; another nursed the

LEFT Black pepper: Vasco da Gama is said to have recouped the costs of his voyage to India in 1497–98 several times over with the proceeds from a single cargo of peppercorns.

BELOW The Botanic Garden at Leyden in 1601. The plants were arranged in order, in their families, as in the pages of an encyclopaedia.

THE APPLIED BOTANIC GARDEN: THE DUTCH AND THE FRENCH

While natural scientists classified plants and investigated their medicinal properties, seeds and roots of many food plants were being transferred from one continent to another. Columbus took European wheat and vines (required for the celebration of the sacraments) to the new world. The Spaniards and Portuguese introduced sugar plants from the Canaries and the Azores to the Caribbean. The reverse movement of American food plants brought Indian corn, or maize, to the Mediterranean, the Near East and India, cassava to West Africa, and potatoes to northern Europe.

These early exchanges took place without passing through a botanic garden. A second kind of garden, the applied colonial botanic garden, came into existence when inter-tropical exchanges began. The Portuguese were the first to round the Cape, enter the Indian Ocean, and reach the fabled spice islands of the Moluccas. In the early 17th century the Dutch ousted the Portuguese, and strove to monopolise the supply of nutmeg and other spices for both medical and culinary uses. Later, they established gardens of

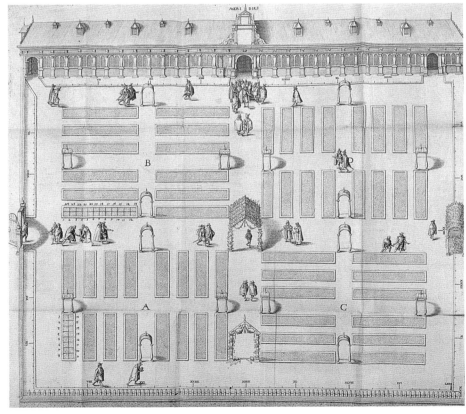

plants when they arrived, built up stocks, and distributed them to the planters. Simultaneously, the mercantile state encouraged the growth of high volume crops, mainly sugar and tobacco at this stage – addictive commodities which could be taxed upon importation to Europe. All these crops were cultivated by slaves brought from Africa, 'the introduction of slaves' being as J-B Dazille said, 'the major and fundamental means for a colony to prosper'. So valuable did the West Indian islands become that wars were fought to win or regain possession of them, and in 1763 critics asserted that the British had made the wrong choice in keeping Canada and returning Guadeloupe to the French at the Treaty of Paris.

THE APPLIED BOTANIC GARDEN: THE BRITISH

In Britain, during the 18th century, one hears less about the state and more about individuals, societies and companies. In 1732 Philip Miller harvested seeds from an East Indian cotton plant in the Apothecaries' Garden at Chelsea and sent them across the Atlantic to Georgia. In 1764 the first British colonial botanic garden was established, in St Vincent, after the Society of Arts offered a reward for anyone setting up an estate in the West Indies where 'the valuable productions of Asia . . . useful in medicine, and profitable as articles of commerce' could be propagated. The garden and the planters received assistance from the Admiralty, which sent Captain Bligh to Tahiti to transfer breadfruit, which was intended as a staple for slaves, to St Vincent. Bligh's first voyage was aborted by the mutiny on the Bounty; his second was

CAMBRIAN

Penrhyn slate
settled from silts
and mudstones
five hundred and twenty million years ago,
bruised purple by so much time.

To roof Europe,
to make floors so cold
the rheum seeped through their bones.
For hearthstone. For dairy slab
where cream was rising gold,

and butter came in the churn, patted
and ridged with a wooden spade
printed with a sheaf of wheat.
Salt-butter left on slate to bead
between the bi-valve of two plates.

Gillian Clarke

LEFT *Sugar canes were taken to the Americas. Like tobacco, which was found there, they were grown on plantations worked by slaves. Harvesting was very heavy labour.*

completed in 1793. But the British government still had no co-ordinated botanical policy, and in 1803 the superintendent of the garden at St Vincent acknowledged that the British were indebted to the French for most of the East Indian plants which they possessed. The one man of vision, Sir Joseph Banks (1743–1820), did not even hold an official appointment. Banks persuaded the East India Company to create a garden at Calcutta in 1787 'for the introduction and propagation of plants important as food, as medicinal sources, or as industrial species of trading significance'. Through his friendship with George III, he built up a collection

of exotic plants in the royal gardens at Kew. In 1789 Kew held 5,800 species. Twenty years later there were 11,000, and the American, South African and Australian floras were particularly well represented.

At the end of the Napoleonic Wars, in 1815, the British kept Ceylon and the Cape which had been captured from the Dutch, and Mauritius which had been taken from the French. The principal gardens of acclimatisation were then in British hands, but the state was slow to grasp the botanical hegemony which lay within its reach. A quarter of a century passed before the Duke of Bedford

(whose estate at Woburn was a botanical garden in all but name) and Professor John Lindley persuaded the government to make Kew into 'the botanical headquarters of the British Empire and its dependencies', which now included New Zealand and its unique flora. In 1841 responsibility for Kew was transferred from the royal to the public purse, and the gardens were enlarged. Few could have guessed that within ten years the first Director, Sir William Hooker, would turn Kew into the leading example of state-led botanical enterprise in the world. In 1865 he was succeeded by his son Joseph, and he in turn by his son-in-law Sir William Turner

ABOVE *The artificial climate in the great Palm House at Kew enabled the Directors to keep the selection and propagation of exotic plants under their own control in London.*

29

at the head of twenty-nine Indian and eighty-three other colonial botanic gardens and field stations almost all of whose superintendents had been trained at Kew and looked to its Director for preferment.

The Directors took over the taxonomic work of the early university botanic gardens. Joseph Hooker co-operated with George Bentham to produce the classic *Genera Plantarum*, and Thiselton-Dyer instituted the *Index Kewensis*, the world's standard list of plants, which is still being revised and expanded to this day as previous identifications have to be corrected and the number of known species continues to rise over a quarter of a million. Sir William Hooker's attempts to promote Kew as a medical garden for London's teaching hospitals foundered in the face of opposition from the Chelsea Physic Garden. The rebuff made little difference. Kew's mission was the development of the productive resources of the empire, or 'economic botany'. Year by year colonial governors were advised that the first duty of their local garden was to keep a living inventory of the native flora, and the second was to act as a conduit through which exchanges could be effected. Everything had to pass through Kew, in order to allow the staff there to establish 'a fixed nomenclature'. On his own initiative, the Director then supplied the colonies with Wardian cases packed with such products of other climes 'as may be deemed suitable for them' – cork oaks to South Australia and pineapples to Brisbane, for example.

Plant transfers were intended to consolidate the position of the United Kingdom as the workshop of the world. Sir William Hooker created a museum or exhibition of the uses of plants for textiles, dyes, gums, and drugs – medicines thus coming back into Kew's operations by another route. Metropolitan manufacturers were invited to inspect the 50,000 named exhibits and pick out the products they could use. The Director identified the most promising varieties of plants to meet their requirements, propagated the stock, and despatched it to the most favourable locations within the Empire, where the subordinate gardens carried out field trials before distributing seeds and seedlings to the planters who were to grow them. Industrialists, planters and importers thus had much of their research and development work done for them. Public money primed the pump of business enterprise.

ABOVE *A headquarters for the British Empire: this building at Kew housed the museum of economic botany in which the many uses of plants were displayed.*

RIGHT *The nutmeg tree was one of the plants transferred by Europeans from the spice islands of the Moluccas in the East Indies to their colonies in the West Indies.*

CINCHONA, RUBBER, CHOCOLATE

RIGHT *The cocoa tree was known to the Mayas and Aztecs. The pods yield both food and drink.*

BELOW *The Cinchona tree, whose bark produces quinine.*

Widespread as the British Empire was, certain useful plants could not be found growing naturally within its borders. These had to be procured. Tea was one example, which a lone agent, Robert Fortune, brought direct from China to India in the 1840s. The best-known case which concerned Kew was cinchona. In the 1850s this plant, which yielded quinine for treating fever, was still a Peruvian monopoly. The British needed it to protect the army of occupation in India against malaria. In 1859–60 the collector Clements Markham smuggled cinchona seeds out of South America. These were sown and germinated and the seedlings grown on at Kew before being sent to India, to be planted among the Nilgiri hills, other

plantations being established in Ceylon and Jamaica. While the cinchona plantations were maturing, rubber was becoming an increasingly important strategic commodity which the Empire must be able to source for itself. The seeds collected from Brazil by Henry Wickham in 1876 were raised at Kew, and transplanted to Ceylon. From there they were forwarded to Malaya and the Straits Settlements where the gardeners at Singapore found out how to tap the latex without injuring the tree. In the 20th century the rubber industry became Kew's greatest achievement. In the meantime cinchona enabled Europeans to penetrate into the interior of West Africa, and this made possible the transfer of yet another American plant, the cocoa tree, and the large-scale production of an additional and seductive luxury, chocolate.

Not every one of Kew's favoured species turned out to be a commercial success. Who now hears of Tussack-grass, from the Falkland Islands, which Sir William Hooker pronounced 'the finest of all grasses for agricultural purposes'? (It turned out that sheep ate the heart out of the plant.) When the historic coffee plantations fell victim to disease, Sir Joseph Hooker advocated substituting the Liberian coffee plant. His successor was obliged to concede that, in the field, harvesting involved 'too much labour and percentage of waste entailed in cleaning'. Cinchona itself was no more than a partial success. Other collectors found higher-yielding varieties, and a British trader, Charles Ledger, spurned by Kew, sold his plants to the Dutch. In the 1920s and 1930s Java supplied ninety per cent of the world market, and the British purchased their quinine in Amsterdam. The Dutch on the other hand obtained their rubber trees from British stock.

THE EUROPEAN DIMENSIONS OF THE BOTANIC GARDEN

University botanic gardens were planted in an attempt to understand the world – upon European terms. In Europe, Latin was the language of the Western Church and of natural science. To other civilisations the idea that the correct name for a plant was the latin one, coupled with the name of the first European to 'discover' it, was an example of European supremacism. It was much the same with medicine. European scientists appropriated

native treatments for dysentery and malaria for their own use. Simultaneously, they dismissed non-European attitudes to sickness as superstitious and fatalistic.

Applied botanic gardens were instruments for the manipulation of nature, managed by European nation states in the imperial stage of their growth. The gardens contributed little to the development of the temperate lands to which Europeans emigrated together with their familiar plants and animals – much to the colonial system of cultivation in the tropics. They cannot, therefore, be dissociated from the bombardments and massacres which stained the European irruption into the waters of the Orient, the traffic in slaves from West Africa, and the quayside auctions in the Americas. Portuguese, Dutch, and British all in turn took the lead in these shameful transactions. By the time the slave trade was outlawed in the 19th century, 10 million human beings had been led away in chains to the New World. Even after abolition, alternative ways of fashioning a dependent workforce were found. Where estates could be cleared, British planters imported indentured Indian labour, as in South Africa and Trinidad, or Chinese coolies, as in Malaysia. Where the peasants were too numerous to be uprooted, as in the jute growing areas of Bengal, or where the Colonial Office wanted to keep them on the land in order to prevent them flocking to the towns, as in West Africa, they had to be persuaded to abandon subsistence agriculture in favour of commodity production. Peasants then became tied to the company as monopoly buyer. These relationships were exploitative, and other more traditional and co-operative methods of production, like the *métayer* system (in which the tenant shares a proportion of the harvest with the land owner), were condemned, even in the Kew Bulletin.

As a result of the botanical exchanges, so many of which were brokered through the botanic garden, vastly increased populations now enjoy varied and more tasty diets, and live longer. Nor have the benefits been monopolised by the Western world. India has given a welcome to plants from every continent. No region has gained more than West Africa, where the introduced maize crops better than the indigenous sorghum and millet, and cassava is the best famine reserve crop. But how to balance these benefits against the evils of the plantation system, the cash crop, and interference with native forest laws? This question is not best answered by the

RIGHT *Henbane contains deadly hyoscyamine. Mercifully, botanic gardens have not developed plant poisons for use in weapons of mass destruction or in hallucination.*

shooting from the ideological hip. But it is one which can be examined from the standpoint of the people of Wales. They, with their compound experience and sense of identity, neither wholly metropolitan nor yet peripheral, are well placed to adjudicate between the colonial legacy and the imperial one.

Both the university botanic gardens and the applied botanic gardens appear to have run their course. The re-creational ideal evaporated in the second half of the 17th century. In the late 19th century taxonomy gradually gave way to the study of plant anatomy and plant physiology. Medication passed into a more mineral-based phase. The applied botanic gardens rose with the empires which they served: with decolonisation they lost their purpose.

Old institutions may adapt. Taxonomy is being reorganised upon DNA principles, and botanic gardens maintain seed banks of endangered species. But conservation can best be undertaken in the field, by taking the botanic garden out into the world – the exact opposite of the principle of bringing the world to the botanic garden with which this story began. In these circumstances there is room for a new foundation to make a fresh start and ask different questions, maybe even, as Kate Soper suggests, crumble away at the ancient but tired distinction between the wilderness and the garden, the natural and the man-made, which is becoming less and less clear-cut with every century that passes.

RIGHT *Cotton began a revolution in personal hygiene through the introduction of cheap, washable underwear.*

33

EARLY DAYS OF THE GARDEN

Andrew Sclater

The landscapes of Wales are enlivened by many great buildings. Mostly ancient and often ruined, they evoke former times, warfare, religion, human endeavour. They are symbols of culture. This chapter tells how a new symbol has emerged in the landscape of Wales.

It was the sensitivity of the artist William Wilkins which changed the fate of the historic landscape at Middleton Hall. Without William, nothing would have happened. The result of the work of so many over a period of eleven years is a grouping of old and new buildings in a landscape that not only astonishes the eye but also provides a cradle for the conservation of plants and for the fusion of old and new in our ways of looking at nature. It is a new physical landmark in Wales and a new intellectual landmark in the world of culture. It happened by awakening Middleton from a slumber of more than fifty years. And when the old place awoke it found itself in a world of new ideas.

William's burning enthusiasm led me to take up the cause too. It was in 1989 that he first shared with me his aspirations for the site. It would have been easy to dismiss them as unattainable – the landscape and buildings of the candidate garden needed so much restoration, and so much that was missing needed to be reinstated: lakes, focal points, paths, and plantings. Converting agricultural grazing into a garden on a vast scale was no small challenge in the middle of rural Carmarthenshire. Inspirationally, William always

spoke in terms of 'when our project succeeds . . .', while I used the more cautious 'if . . .'.

THE REDISCOVERY OF MIDDLETON

Our story begins with an aunt and a country estate that had almost vanished. The year was 1987. The late Miss Rose Powell visited the woods at Middleton Hall with a party of naturalists, and returned to report the survival of a number of interesting structures to her nephew William Wilkins. On his first visit to Middleton, William realised that the estate had been designed to 18th-century ideals of beauty. Although it was, or had been, a work of art, pervasive decay or outright destruction blighted it. Nevertheless, if the remnants were pieced together, a work of great ambition suggested itself. What is more, the very abandonment that had caused this decay had also prevented any fundamental alteration of the setting which Sir William Paxton had laid out during the 1790s. Two hundred years on, Middleton acquired a new champion in William Wilkins, but how would the landowner react to the interests of this outsider?

Unsurprisingly, the Middleton Hall estate was no longer in private hands. After the First World War, the County Council had acquired its 568 acres of parkland and, in 1931, it added the site of the former Hall, soon after it had tragically burnt to the ground. The houses of Paxton's tenants had been modernised by the

OPPOSITE *Middleton Hall, back view, painted in 1853 by Augustus Butler. The hill on which the Hall once stood is now crowned by Lord Foster's Glasshouse.*

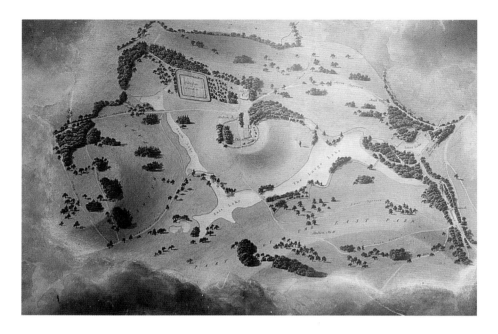

ABOVE *A bird's-eye view of the picturesque landscape park at Middleton, painted by Thomas Hornor for Sir William Paxton in 1815, 20 years after the Hall was built.*

council, and the land sub-divided into small farm units. By the mid 1980s, many of the Middleton farms were becoming too small to be viable. Social and economic change was once again casting a long shadow over the future. Farming in Carmarthenshire in the 1980s no longer promised the wealth that had made the Tywi Valley famous for its dairy production earlier in the century. Thus, when William raised the question of a new future for Middleton to the officers of Dyfed County Council in 1989, he was given a hearing. It is fortunate indeed that the Council was ready to contemplate a new vision for Middleton.

THE GERMINATING IDEA

Ideas and proposals were needed, and so William invited me to form and chair the Middleton Steering Group. As the landscape was 'too far gone' and Wales, at the time, had no scheme of grant aid for conserving and restoring historic landscapes, the proposal to create a garden capable of attracting paying visitors offered a serious and, just possibly, realistic prospect for the place. After all, the estate could not be saved unless it could generate enough money by itself, or a new and sustainable plan could be devised for it. We talked initially of a restored garden of 'botanical calibre' and Middleton became a prime focus for the Welsh Historic Gardens Trust, formed by William Wilkins in 1989. A nucleus of

its founder members worked in the Steering Group with great dedication to define aims and develop initiatives during the early years of 1989 and 1990. From 1992, the Trust increasingly distanced itself from the Middleton project, as plans emerged that arguably had more to do with creating a new garden than with conserving an old one.

Two people played a critical early role in strengthening a collective resolve to rescue the estate from oblivion. First came Brian Morris, then Principal of St David's University College at Lampeter and now Lord Morris of Castle Morris. He was taken to Middleton, and listened to William Wilkins extolling the qualities of its landscape. Those qualities were not easy to convey to others, who often saw only a threadbare fabric. With his painter's eye, William was never in any doubt about them, though. His view was not without precedent – the estate had been commended, in John Claudius Loudon's great gazetteer of parks in 1826, as:

'One of the most splendid mansions in South Wales, by Cockrell; the grounds finely planted, and containing an elegant prospect-tower, and a good kitchen-garden.'

In tune with Loudon and several other commentators, Brian Morris responded enthusiastically and encouraged bolder and more ambitious thinking about its future.

The next visitor of consequence was a new council member of the Welsh Historic Gardens Trust, Professor Sir Ghillean Prance, Director of the Royal Botanic Gardens at Kew. He put us in touch with someone who considered it scandalous that Wales had no National Botanic Garden: Edmund de Rothschild, owner of the great rhododendron collection at Exbury in Hampshire. When, in due course, Professor Prance and Mr de Rothschild affirmed their belief that Middleton was the place to make a National Botanic Garden, it was not difficult to arrange for them to meet the owners, Dyfed County Council, and its chief executive, D H Davies, who staunchly supported our ideas.

At that moment began a quest for something that had not been contemplated in the British Isles for nearly two centuries – the creation of a new botanic garden to represent a nation, its concern for plants and their importance to humanity. Such a project was

ABOVE *The Tywi Valley – the inspiring landscape in which the idea of the National Botanic Garden took root.*

LEFT *Paxton's tower – the 'elegant prospect tower' noted by John Claudius Loudon – from the direction where the Great Glasshouse now stands.*

37

PRE-CAMBRIAN

Vertiginous numbers:
seven hundred million years.

Granite from Anglesey. Is it this
we tread on, this starry pavement,

a glittering milky way underfoot?
Take one in your hand,

a paving sett to turn under the light
so small and heavy it can teach you gravity.

Gillian Clarke

'unheard of' in our time: Scotland had inaugurated its national botanic garden at Edinburgh in 1670; England and Ireland had created theirs, at Kew and Glasnevin respectively, in the mid and late 18th century. But Wales had never had one nor, apparently, had it ever voiced any particular need for one.

Supporters had to be won far and wide. We had to convince others that a botanic garden was required in Wales, and would supply the sustainable use that Middleton needed. While press and television coverage burgeoned, more and more requests for talks came in from community groups and clubs, and hundreds of meetings were held. A rich vision of a garden was presented: one that celebrated connections between Wales and its plants, between traditional agriculture and contemporary practices of conservation, and which brought scientific and cultural perspectives together. If voyages of discovery and foreign conquest provided the context of earlier botanic gardens, what cultural trends in today's world would connect with our new botanic garden? Whatever the answer was to be, the vital, burning excitement we felt must have been

an important part of the founding of earlier botanic gardens too. We were in touch with a tradition.

The challenges we faced in defining our purpose were surely similar to those faced by our forerunners. Their gardens were shaped by attitudes towards plants as commodities and objects of economic value. In our time, 'green' values have brought with them a new respect for natural organisms, and introduced moral questions about the exploitation of nature. Meanwhile, many now see science as more to do with artifice than with knowledge of nature. The new botanic garden must mark this sea-change in our attitudes and respond by carrying messages far beyond the old confines of the laboratory, the conservatories and the botanical order beds. Such a garden should bring together knowledge and inspiration, formerly segregated into different disciplines that seldom exchanged information between them. In the tradition of one of Wales' great thinkers, the late Raymond Williams, who re-evaluated the relationship between society and the countryside, the new garden could review our relations with nature itself. As science has resoundingly demonstrated that plants are the essential support to all other life on earth, the botanic garden of tomorrow had the potential to bring plants out of the scientific closet, to resume their time-honoured place as essential co-habitees of the planet. The plants in such a garden would appeal to everyone, whether specialist or not, if the garden could interact with all of the ways in which we experience and think about plants and the wider natural environment.

DEVELOPING STRENGTH

In 1990 four documents which reinforced the project's credibility were produced. These were my *Preliminary Feasibility Study*, the *Concept Appraisal: a botanic garden for the 21st century* by Michael Maunder of Kew, the *Project Orientation* by Stephen Kember, and Christopher Gallagher's *Historic Landscape Survey*.

Good ideas have a way of generating rivals. We learned of the plans of other gardens in Wales to compete as sites for the National Botanic Garden. Accordingly, we invited leading botanists from Wales and elsewhere to a meeting in Brecon in 1991. Those present included representatives of colleges of the University of Wales, as well as the National Museum and Galleries

OPPOSITE *A farm in Snowdonia National Park – now conservation is an issue for all the countryside, not just in spectacular areas like this.*

of Wales, and Professor Prance who chaired the meeting. Our message was clear: we sought to complement and strengthen the opportunities for botany in Wales by establishing a National Botanic Garden at Middleton. We wanted to raise the profile of a scientific discipline that had too long been overshadowed by more technological, as well as more theoretical, subjects. The meeting proved fruitful. There was a sense that the garden we proposed would have a vital role to play. A quorum of Welsh botanists supported the launching of our ambitious botanical ark, albeit into uncharted waters.

And there were detractors too. Letters were written to the press by a local pressure group which saw the project as destructive of the environment. Others challenged the need for a new garden when older ones in Wales were suffering from lack of funds. Controversy was in the air. There was much talk of a 'Welsh Kew' – a useful enough soundbite. But we would miss our point completely if we were simply to be a clone of Kew. After all, we were going to be more modern by two whole centuries and would have more space, more rain and cleaner air. It was a new generation of botanic garden that was to be advocated – a 'physic garden' for an astrophysic age. Respect for the environment was at the project's core.

COMPETITION AND COMPLICATION

When the council's Director of Planning, David Bown, accepted the chair of the Steering Group in 1991, we gained tangible proof not only of the council's support, but also of the landowner's faith. Meanwhile, dedicated enthusiasts like the never-tiring Aberystwyth botanist, John Savidge, provided essential technical support. A Working Group was formed. There were now separate teams to scale different faces of the mountain in a strategy to reach the summit ahead of any rival.

Later in 1991 the Burgess Partnership's *Feasibility Study* confirmed that the concept of a new botanic garden at Middleton was viable, but there was still no clear source of funding. Someone had to be employed to dedicate serious professional time, or we would lose momentum. I proposed William Wilkins who accepted the challenge. His new brief was to develop the project to the point at which it could attract capital funding.

In 1994 an independent charitable trust was established to oversee the project. Those willingly accepting to become trustees were chosen from the worlds of business, the professions, government, and academic botany, including Dianne Edwards from the University of Wales, Ghillean Prance of Kew Gardens, and Robin Herbert, President of the Royal Horticultural Society. B K Thomas, a Cardiff businessman, became the Trust's first chairman. Through Professor Prance, successive Secretaries of State were introduced to the concept of a botanic garden and its role in the late 20th century. The first, David Hunt, was very responsive and encouraging. The omens looked promising, but Mr Hunt was soon replaced by John Redwood in a cabinet re-shuffle.

Fortunes seemed to be waning in the autumn of 1994 when the unconvinced John Redwood called for an extensive study to examine the need for a Welsh botanic garden. After inviting all local authorities to propose alternative sites, he concluded that Middleton was not unique as a suitable site: Clyne Gardens in Swansea, Bute Park in Cardiff, and Penhein in Gwent were also acceptable. Since Welsh Office funding would not be forthcoming, there was no need to declare any site the outright winner.

So, the Middleton team, having promoted the original concept of a National Botanic Garden, henceforth had to compete in a 'free for all'. The contest to be entered was soon announced: the newly formed Millennium Commission was seeking proposals for landmark projects to be completed in the year 2000. Without their support, in the form of National Lottery money, it was evident that there would be no botanic garden, and so much work would have been in vain. But we were no longer alone with our idea – we would have to challenge rival bids from Swansea and from Gwent.

PURSUING MILLENNIUM POSSIBILITIES

The glorious weather and marquee reception that greeted the commissioners arriving at Middleton in the summer of 1995 suggested pastoral tranquility rather than desperation. But the coming of the Commission created unforeseen demands and expectations of the project. First, encouragement by the Commission to increase the overall capital value to £43 million could be interpreted as a vote of support, but the grants would

OPPOSITE *New plantings on the south-facing hillside below the Great Glasshouse.*

ABOVE *Architecture and landscape design in harmony.*

work together for the first time at Middleton, producing a glorious fusion of landscape and architecture, history and modernity. The aesthetics of the garden were in safe hands.

The business side proved to be equally well served. The consultants were subjected to review after review as the Millennium Commission scrutinised costings, assessed public support, and minutely examined the business plan, fundraising strategy, and land acquisition issues, often imposing apparently new and unattainable targets during a gruelling fifteen months. Valiantly, the documents were polished and perfected until every question had been satisfactorily answered.

Eventually, some £9 million was either promised or well within the project team's sights. Carmarthenshire County Council promised to lease the estate on a 999-year peppercorn rent – a munificent gift representing private funding to the tune of some £2 million. The application was formally submitted in October 1995, before either of its rivals. On December 12, instead of a result, came the disheartening news that the application was deferred. Had this undone Middleton's advantage? Was the Millennium Commission awaiting the rival bids? Worry was in the air, the outlook seemed bleak. The Commission had proved it could be hard, having just declared that it would not support the great Cardiff Bay Opera House project.

In January 1996 trustees Dan Clayton-Jones, Robin Herbert, Alan Haywood, and Rod Thurman met Jenny Page of the Commission to discuss concerns regarding the occupancy of several houses on the estate, and the amount of money raised by the project team. It was agreed that no compulsory purchases would be made to acquire properties, and that the project would be split into two phases of equal financial value. This eased the immediate problems of fundraising, as Phase I could proceed when the Garden had raised a quarter of the total project value rather than a half as previously required. But there was a sting in the Commission's tail: the project team soon faced a deadline of just three weeks to secure promises of a further £1 million to equalise the Garden's contribution and the Phase I Millennium offer. The key £1 million came from Dŵr Cymru-Welsh Water, whose chairman, Brian Charles, later became Deputy Chairman of the Botanic Garden.

After seven years of intense labour and persistence, all who had

cover just half of the money. That left about £21.5 million to be found by the project team. Secondly, there would be no grant for running costs, so the business plan had to be honed to require no subsidy. And financial viability had to be proven. Furthermore, local government in Wales was to be reorganised, and our stalwart benefactor, Dyfed County Council, was to be disbanded. Roderic Morgan, Chief Executive of Carmarthen District Council, which took on Dyfed County Council's work in Carmarthenshire, joined the Steering Group. Both he and his authority vigorously supported the project and gave splendid assistance during the run-up to a Millennium application that cost £300,000 to prepare.

That application depended upon first-class designers and experts from a wide range of professions. The existing team of consultants were augmented by Ilex Leisure, KPMG management consultants, Friedland fundraising specialists and the lawyers Edwards Geldard. Extraordinary generosity was shown, with many agreeing to be paid only if the project succeeded, and others offering all or part of their services for free. Among the most exciting work were the proposals for buildings by Norman Foster's practice, and designs for the landscape by Colvin and Moggridge. These firms, assisted by Symonds the quantity surveyors, came to wonderful news of success, conveyed by Michael Heseltine together with similar good news for the Arms Park Stadium. The Millennium Commission grant of £21.7 million to the National Botanic Garden of Wales was officially announced to the public on 1 March 1996.

DREAM TO REALITY

In a sense the work was only just beginning. The trustees, having overseen developments since 1994, now had to plan for the making of the reality. While contracts were being drawn up, in July 1996, HRH The Prince of Wales made a tour of the site, to see for himself the location and scope of the project to which William Wilkins had first introduced him on the royal train in North Wales some five years earlier. By the end of the summer, contracts had been signed. The birth of the garden was inevitable. The Garden's first Director, Professor Charles Stirton, arrived at Middleton late in 1996 from the Royal Botanic Gardens, Kew, where he had been Deputy Director.

Work began on site in spring 1997. Simultaneously, new ideas and detail were added to the founding ethos. Policy statements were produced for the arts, education, health, and for the way in which the site would be managed. These were all linked by the common principles of sustainable development and preferred futures. Under Charles Stirton, the philosophy of the Botanic Garden has come to encompass not only the principle that sustainability is fundamental to survival, but also an acknowledgement that we must consider how it is that we prefer to manage the planet into the future, and at a local level how we choose to manage the daily business of our lives with a view to our collective futures.

Many fundraising events were held in Wales and London, hosted by the Society of Apothecaries, the Mexican Embassy, and Wales in London among others. At Middleton Hall, the old agricultural landscape remained little changed, except for the huge hole excavated for the foundations of the Great Glasshouse. In spring 1998, Ron Davies, the then Labour Secretary of State for Wales, joined the Garden's new Chairman, Dan Clayton-Jones, and former Millennium Commission Chief Executive Eric Sorensen to bury a time capsule in the footings of the building, which was completed by October.

The year 1998 was crucial to securing the transition to Phase II. Having met the Phase I funding targets, and achieved major construction goals, the Garden secured the commitment of the Millennium Commission for funding to take the project forward. During 1999, important contributions were received from the Principality Building Society (for the Lifelong Learning Centre), Wales Tourist Board (for visitor facilities), and from the European Regional Development Fund (for visitor facilities and science).

At the close of the second millennium, the final good news was that HRH The Prince of Wales accepted to become the Patron of the National Botanic Garden. It would not have been possible to find a more prestigious endorsement than that of the royal leader of Wales, himself a dedicated champion of environmental sensitivity and lover of plants and gardens. He shares the aspirations of the Garden, and will certainly help to uphold values of sustainability and respect for nature.

Now that the National Botanic Garden finally exists, Wales has gained a cultural institution the like of which it has never seen before. The Garden ranks with institutions like the National Library and the National Museum and Galleries of Wales as a centrepiece of Welsh culture. But it also joins the worldwide family of botanic gardens: a family which has failed to produce many children in the 20th century. The National Botanic Garden of Wales gives new blood to this family.

As you look across the patchwork of traditional pastures, your first impression of this garden will be of an extraordinary and unexpected new landmark in rural Wales. A landmark devoted to life: the lives of plants and the future of life on earth.

BELOW *Nature and culture: contrast and complement.*

PLAN
LAND

TS AND
SCAPE

THE PLANTS IN THE GARDEN

Ivor Stokes

OPPOSITE Protea
neriifolia *grows to 3*
metres in height in the
South African fynbos from
Cape Town to Port

RIGHT *A view across The*
Broadwalk with herbaceous
plants and a mature purple
beech dominating the scene.

The great botanic gardens of the world are as much a reflection of the time of their creation as they are of the interests of their owners or designers.

Parterres and wildernesses take their place alongside the many arboreta that celebrate the grand age of botanical exploration during the latter part of the 19th century and the early decades of the 20th century. We rightly cherish the many fine examples and exotic collections, from that period, that survive to this day. Yet mankind's relationship with nature has changed and, with that change, our understanding of ecology and plant sciences has grown. No longer do we develop our botanic gardens as if we were building a stamp collection, bringing together the latest introductions to allow us to marvel at the diversity and bountifulness of nature. No more do we arrogantly exploit plants of economic value by moving them around the world at our whim, without a thought to giving anything back to the people who rightly have genetic sovereignty over them or to the potential damage such introductions inflict on the natural flora. The Convention on Biological Diversity and international CITES (Convention on International Trade in Endangered Species of Wild Flora and Fauna) legislation have put an end to all that.

The focus, now, has moved to more pressing matters, with conservation and education being at the forefront of any modern garden's activities. That is not to say that the amenity aspects of the plants fail to get consideration. Exotic plants certainly exist in the National Botanic Garden of Wales, in their thousands, but many of them are presented for visitors to enjoy in more naturalistic settings than have hitherto been created.

PLANTS AND LANDSCAPE

THE WOODLANDS OF THE WORLD

A low hill, just to the south of the centre of the site, is our Woodlands of the World, wherein areas of threatened temperate rainforests, from places with similar climates to that of West Wales, are being planted. We are using seed and young plants of known wild origin, ensuring that a wide a range of variants of each species is represented so that they have a high conservation value. These woodlands vary in size from 0.2 of a hectare/½ an acre to 1.6–2 hectares/4 or 5 acres in extent. They include everything from the dominant tree species, down through the shrub layer to the herbaceous plants that run through the leaf litter on the forest floor. Visitors will walk through a 'Chinese' woodland in May and gasp at the beauty of the *Magnolia* and *Rhododendron* species in flower. Above them the new foliage of the graceful conifers, snake-bark maples and dove trees will be expanding, whilst at their feet *Corydalis*, and *Primula* species will be blooming with a host of other flowers. Across a grassy glade, the visitor will be confronted with 'Chile' in the spring. Monkey puzzle trees, Southern beech and *Fitzroya* will tower above *Embothrium coccineum* – the 'flame trees', the unusual *Desfontainea* and golden-flowered *Berberis*. Twined through their branches will be the beautiful *Lapageria rosea*, with its pendulous lily-like flowers.

These plantings are being undertaken using trees that are currently just a metre or so in height and in some cases even smaller. Most of these plants have been donated to the Garden by other institutions in Britain as part of their programmes of disseminating surplus seedlings, others have been raised from seed recently collected on expeditions around the world. It will be many years before they achieve maturity and resemble their counterparts in far-off lands. We are planting these woodlands for the next generation and the one beyond.

The chosen site is somewhat exposed, and to assist the young plants in their establishment, we are planting many hundreds of temporary 'nurse trees' to protect them from the extremes of the weather. Once we are sure our wild-collected plants can hold their own, their guardians will be removed to allow them the space to develop freely. The resulting timber will be either sawn and converted to useful planks or become fuel-chips for the Biomass boiler.

ABOVE *Ivor Stokes,
Director of Horticulture,
with 'grass trees' waiting
in the nursery glasshouses
for their final move.*

OPPOSITE Araucaria
araucana, *the 'monkey
puzzle', growing in its
native habitat of Chile.*

LEFT *The snake-bark maple*
Acer davidii *brings
splashes of colour to an
autumn woodland in
Yunnan, South West China.*

49

THE MOORLANDS OF THE WORLD

A similar 'phytogeographical' theme to that of the Woodlands underscores the Moorlands of the World, an area we plan to create on a nearby hill with natural outcrops of Old Red Sandstone. This area will be established once the Science Centre has been completed and will extend over the roofs of the building. Here, resisting an inevitably artificial looking rock garden, we will plant large drifts of plants that are found in the sub-alpine heathlands above the treeline in many areas of the world. Plants from countries as diverse as Tasmania and Lesotho are being brought together for the first time in cultivation. Like the plants in the Woodlands of the World, these too are of known provenance, so giving a scientific as well as an amenity value to the plantings. The Moorlands of the World, with their dwarf shrubs and low herbaceous plants, will reach maturity more quickly than the Woodlands.

RIGHT *A moorland of the southern hemisphere — Mawson's plateau, Rodway Range, Tasmania.*

BORDER, STEPPES AND PRAIRIES

Herbaceous plants reach maturity within a year or two of their seed being sown, and our earliest visitors will be greeted with an established border running between The Broadwalk and the eastern perimeter of the Walled Garden. This 'traditional' herbaceous border is 230 metres/250 yards long, and potentially of a depth that is too great to allow the plants at the back to be appreciated. To overcome this, a network of small paths has been constructed which enables our visitors to disappear into a lushness of flowers and foliage to experience all the plants at close quarters. The herbaceous plants in this area have been themed with complementary and contrasting colours to give breathtaking displays over a long period. Among the plants are young trees and shrubs that give a framework to the border during the winter months, when the herbaceous material has mostly died down. Winter flowers of *Hamamelis* and *Viburnum* with the coloured barks of *Acer*, *Betula* and *Cornus* ensure that there is something eye-catching whatever the season.

In contrast to this border, and a similar herbaceous scheme on a south-facing slope situated alongside one of the lakes, we have created an innovative type of extensive planting that has not been undertaken previously in Britain on such a scale. An area of more than 3.2 hectares/8 acres will be transformed into a representation of an American prairie or a Central European steppe. Innovation is a word that is heard frequently at the National Botanic Garden of Wales. However, to be innovative one has to be willing to accept the possibility of failure. The mild, moist climate of West Wales differs greatly from that of the continental climates which have allowed the steppes and prairies to evolve. Although many of their constituent flowering plants thrive in a closely tended, traditional herbaceous border, it is a different matter to try to create an analogue of these habitats themselves, where the plants are able to thrive in a state of happy equilibrium with their neighbours.

RIGHT *The stunning colour of* Acer palmatum *foliage in late autumn.*

One of the most common causes of failure is the invasive nature of the strong-growing native grasses that quickly smother the introduced species, so that the area soon reverts to the appearance of a neglected field. To overcome this, we have stripped off the topsoil from the site, in the hope that we have removed most of the dormant native seeds with it. This has, additionally, lowered the fertility which will deter any fresh weed seeds from establishing themselves before the desired herbaceous plants are of a size where they can hold their own against competition. The lack of soil fertility is of little concern, for in their natural habitats many of these herbaceous plants are found growing in dry, stony soils. The individual plants may not achieve the dimensions that they would in a manured and dug border, but here they do not require staking and constant attention to give of their best. Drifts of ornamental grasses complement the plantings and give a pleasing effect to the area in winter, when their foliage and seed heads assume subtle hues of beige and bronze.

THE DOUBLE WALLED GARDEN

Adjacent to The Broadwalk is the Walled Garden. It is, we believe, unique within Wales in that it consists of two concentric walls, barely 9 metres/10 yards apart. The recently restored outer wall is constructed solely of stone, whilst the inner wall is of brick and stands to a somewhat greater height.

The differing heat-retentive qualities of brick and stone are well known and many gardens throughout history have incorporated brick in their south-facing walls to give extra warmth to the plants growing against them, and to encourage the ripening of their exotic fruits. Rarely did garden designers go as far as to build two complete enclosures out of each material on the same site. Like so many other walled gardens, ours had an internal perimeter path with further cruciform paths quartering the area under cultivation, and meeting at the fountain and dipping pool in the centre. It also boasted a peach house and ancillary buildings. During the last 60 or so years it has experienced uses that were at odds with the preservation of the fabric and features built by Sir William Paxton 200 years ago. As a one-time market garden, the whole internal area, paths and all, was ploughed on a regular basis. More recently, it became a safe grazing area for cattle.

The lack of interest or investment in the infrastructure during this period enabled 'mother nature', who rarely shows respect for human handiwork, to quietly reclaim the area. Wind- and bird-sown seeds, germinating between the bricks and stones on the top of the wall, soon pushed their roots down to loosen the hold of the old lime mortar. Several large stretches of the walls had collapsed to become grass-covered mounds. Little remains of the fabric of the peach house, but a recent limited archaeological

OPPOSITE *The crumbling fabric of the Walled Garden, with the Peach House in the distance — awaiting the skill of the restorer's hand.*

EL NINO IN THE WALLED GARDEN

*The moon and planets step out in a row
along the moon-road. Close doors. Draw curtains now.
The wild child's fists are full of snow.*

*Somewhere on earth this year there are no birds,
no wing-beat in the breeding-grounds, no herds
of travelling buffalo, no words*

*to weigh the heaviest blizzard ever known,
the worst tornado flattening little towns,
the slash and burn that brings great forests down.*

*Let the skylark sing its heart out in the air.
Let the moon reflect in the wide-awake eye of the hare
asleep in its form. Let the otter come home to the river.*

*It's time to get it right, to create Eden
from a wilderness in a walled garden.*

Gillian Clarke

standards'. We have incorporated many of the named varieties of hazel that are fast disappearing with the grubbing-up of uneconomical nut plats (as hazel plantations are traditionally called), along with a large collection of snowdrop varieties, donated by the late Primrose Warburg. The area is a delight to visit in early spring when the rest of the Garden is still thinking about responding to the increasing hours of daylight.

The necklace of five lakes, that are in the main area of the Garden, present unequalled opportunities for displaying waterlilies and other aquatic plants on a scale that is not to be found in any other British botanic garden. The margin of one of these lakes abuts part of the Woodlands of the World and here we have the opportunity to grow some of the plants that require a higher moisture content in the soil than we can provide on the hillside. The other margins host a range of both native and exotic plants that enjoy having their roots in water and provide invaluable cover for many invertebrates and other riparian animals.

BELOW The Hybrid Nymphaea 'Gloire du Temple sur Lot', bred by Joseph Latour-Marliac who revolutionised the waterlily and died in 1911 without revealing the secrets of his technique.

excavation has shown that it possessed a sophisticated hypocaust heating system, with flue walls and slated pathways to contain the planting beds for the fruit and other ornamental plants that would once have been cherished there.

The innovation that Paxton employed in creating his house and garden at Middleton must surely dictate the Garden's approach to this feature. Throughout West Wales there are several walled gardens from the same period in a far finer state of repair, and there is little point in attempting to recreate yet another, especially as we do not have the benefit of any written archive to tell us what was originally there. The absence of any major surviving elements within the Walled Garden gives us the opportunity to start with a clean sheet and create a landscape that reflects the history, function and design of walled gardens in a global context, whilst respecting and restoring what little remains of the original fabric.

To the west of the Walled Garden is an area of semi-natural woodland, on the flank of a small hill. It gives some degree of protection from the prevailing westerly winds and provides a useful elevated area from which to look down into the Walled Garden. This woodland has suffered from lack of management in recent years, and the ground flora is losing its richness with the encroachment of such species as sycamore, blackthorn and bramble. Volunteers and students from our local college have adopted this area and have cleared the dense undergrowth, creating a network of paths and turning the woodland into a 'coppice with

BELOW *Ripening olives —
an important food
plant grown in all the
mediterranean zones.*

ABOVE *A Californian
hillside showing the
preference of the plants for
the sheltered slopes away
from the wind and sun.*

THE MEDITERRANEAN CLIMATE
IN WALES

However wonderful, inspiring or innovative our various designs
and plantings, whatever messages we want our visitors to take
home with them about the importance of plants to life on this
planet, the lasting image of any visit to the National Botanic Garden
of Wales is surely that of the Great Glasshouse, at the very heart
of the site.

The Garden's Great Glasshouse must surely rank as one of
the finest, if not the finest and most elegant, glasshouse in the
world. The horticultural team at the Garden has worked closely
with the designers in order to create as natural a landscape as
possible within this exciting space. There are no formal pathways
within the landscape – visitors are therefore not confined to a
ribbon of concrete as they walk through the plantings, as is so
often the case with other gardens. The entire surface is
covered with light-coloured sandstone rocks and chippings

OLEA EUROPA

'Like gold', they'd say of the oil in the two ounce bottle
from the chemist, kept in the medicine cupboard.
They'd warm the drops and let them, bead by bead,
into the sounding pain of a child's ear.
Warmed oil of olives, and the spell was cast.

If they could see us now as we dip our bread
in saucers of extra-virgin, green-gold oil
bought by the litre, lick our fingers clean
then slip the oval fruits into our mouths,
taking the flesh till there's nothing left but the stone.

*

From Granada, eighteenth century Spain,
a grove of olives leaning in a shed,
their gauze drawn back, like veils,
roots still bound in gesso for the journey,
sipping moisture from it as they need.

Even here they are Mediterranean,
their stillness animal, limbs creased
at the joints, skin stretched silver
under the bark. They hold time
in the heartwood as rock does.

Their darkness makes an aura out of light,
a painting by Cézanne, where rock, tree, sky
burn with the negatives of sun and stone,
black branches and the smoking silver of leaves
wreathed in a grove of olives and wild flowers.

Under glass, two-hundred-year-old trees
slowly, slowly grow towards the light,
the almost midnight sunsets of midsummer,
temperate Atlantic winter skies
in a saucer of glass between hills and rain.

Gillian Clarke

of various sizes. Amongst the plants there are larger stones, small rocks and even boulders. Where there are no plantings, these uneven surfaces grade down to fine chippings that have been compacted to provide a firm walking surface which is accessible to both wheelchairs and the heavy equipment that is needed to maintain the internal fabric of the structure. The impression is therefore that one is in fact walking through a real landscape, since there are no formal edges to separate the people from the plants.

Another difference is that the whole of this space is dedicated to growing plants from the mediterranean climate areas of the world. There are five areas of the globe that can be said to have mediterranean climates. They lie between latitudes 30 and 45 degrees north and south of the equator on west-facing coasts and comprise the Western Cape in South Africa, the southwestern part of Western Australia and the southernmost part of the state of South Australia, central Chile, the region to the west of the Sierra Nevada in California and, of course, most of the Mediterranean

ABOVE *A close-up of*
Protea cynaroides, *the*
national flower of
South Africa.

easily be confused with the many species of *Erica* that also occur in the Fynbos, only distinguishing themselves when they bear their flowers. Amongst the rocks beneath all these low shrubs is a wealth of bulbs — the Western Cape is home to the greatest variety of bulbous plants in the world. Across the terraces is a large area representing Australia. The vegetation of the Kwongan is similar in form to that of the South African Fynbos, despite being separated by several thousand miles of ocean. (Both regions have several plant families in common with Chile, a reminder of the days when the three continents formed part of the super-continent of Gondwana which was centred on the South Pole.)

The 'Ericoid' shrubs of Western Australia, with their small needle-like leaves, include many genera such as *Kunzea*, *Melaleuca*, *Callitris* and *Darwinia* within the myrtle family, and, like their counterparts in South Africa, are often indistinguishable from one another until they are in flower. Emerging through these low drifts of shrubs are species of *Xanthorrhoea*, the 'grass trees', slow-growing ancient plants with fire-blackened trunks, as well as various multi-stemmed, shrubby *Eucalyptus* species known as 'Mallees', which are very different from the tall, graceful trees that we normally associate with the genus. At the eastern end of the Glasshouse, mature olives and pomegranates rise above the dwarf palms (*Chamaerops*), *Cistus*, *Retama*, rosemary, lavenders and sage that are so typical of the flora of the Mediterranean Basin. On the southern side of the Glasshouse, nearest to the glass itself, are the zones dedicated to Chile and California. The vegetation of the 'Matorral', Coastal Sagebrush and 'Chapparal' in these countries closely resembles that of the Mediterranean Basin and includes many species such as *Ceanothus*, *Ribes*, *Lithraea* and *Escallonia*. These species are of borderline hardiness in the British Isles and are often seen in sheltered gardens. Despite their familiarity in the UK, they are included here in order to complete the picture of the unique flora of the mediterranean climate areas of the world.

Basin. Between them they cover just 1.7% of the earth's surface and yet they contain over 20% of the world's known species of flowering plants.

Human pressures from urban development, agriculture, recreation and invasive introductions in these areas have put much of the flora here under threat, especially as there is an extremely high degree of endemism, with many plants having a very limited distribution. The climate is an attractive one with warm to hot summers and the rain comes during the cooler winter months. Many of these plants will be totally unfamiliar to our visitors, but nonetheless they are of great beauty and of interesting form. Since these plants grow most actively during the rainy winter season, they are a challenge to cultivate successfully in Britain, as light levels here are a lot lower than they are in the natural mediterranean habitats.

The arrangement of the space within the Glasshouse has allowed us to follow the same phytogeographical presentation as we are undertaking externally. The plants from each of these areas are grouped together in as natural an association as we·can portray. In the section devoted to South Africa, *Protea*, *Mimetes* and *Leucadendron* species mingle with the reed-like Restionaceae. In foliage, plants of the genera *Coleonema*, *Diosma* and *Agathosma* can

CONSERVATION AND COMMUNITY

The conservation work of the Garden is not confined to exotic plants; modern botanic gardens are increasingly being urged to champion their native flora. With the many thousands of people who visit gardens, botanic gardens are ideally situated to inform

OPPOSITE *'Grass trees'* —
Xanthorrhoea *sp.*
seen in full splendour
amongst the Kwongan
vegetation in South
West Australia.

their visitors of the importance of conserving the native plants which have evolved in the localities where they naturally grow. Human pressures of agriculture and urbanisation are as much a threat to the plants of Wales as they are to plants anywhere else in the world. It is surprising to many people to learn that of its 1,500 species of native plants, Wales has 84 species entered in the Red Data book of threatened plants.

With 160 hectares/400 acres of species-rich woodland and parkland within its perimeter, the National Botanic Garden of Wales is in a unique position to demonstrate sustainable agricultural practices, maintaining and even enhancing the biodiversity that it has inherited. The use of chemicals is avoided in these areas as it is in our horticultural operations. As a developing institution, the Garden is able to implement the sustainability elements of 'Local Agenda 21', which arose from the 1992 Rio Earth Summit. Design guidelines were issued to all the architects, designers, consultants and contractors associated with the project, outlining the philosophy that was to underpin the development of the Garden as well as its future operation. Wherever possible, consideration is given to the source of all the materials that are used. The use of waste or recycled products and locally sourced materials is encouraged, whether it is for our composts, fuels or buildings.

The expertise that is found within the community has been given freely to the Garden in the development and implementation of its various policies, be they in education, transport, estate management, science, arts, health or horticulture. A Community Liaison Group has been established to keep our neighbours abreast of developments and address any concerns that they may have. Volunteers form a valuable part of the Garden's labour force, assisting in administration, gardening activities, and acting as guides. In return, we offer training and skills enhancement along with a good social atmosphere. Through all these dedicated supporters the long term future of the Garden is assured – it is their garden as much as it is ours.

Having spent more than thirty years in the gardening fraternity and having travelled widely during that time, I am convinced that this is the most exciting development in horticulture and botanic gardens the world will see for many a year to come.

THE 'GENIUS' AND HISTORIES OF MIDDLETON

Andrew Sclater

We do not only see landscapes, we use our senses to feel them too. Today's emphasis on the visual has given special weight to the look of a place, but the expression 'looks aren't everything' rings particularly true for landscapes. Knowledge as well as the senses plays a supporting part in our experience. As any tourist will know, it adds a further dimension: if you learn something about a place – its history, people associated with it, its economy, and sometimes its future prospects – you start to think about it differently. You may end up actually seeing it differently too.

MIDDLETON AND THE SENSES

Let me begin by sharing with you an experience of mine at Middleton. It is a damp, quiet, grey day, typical of the Tywi Valley in early spring or autumn. It's not too cold, but your coat is fastened, rain threatens. Sheep bleat in nearby farms, dogs bark, a tractor passes. The buzzard mews in the sky. The sound of someone hammering travels across the fields and seems to be softly wrapped in a huge outer silence. This is a land where sharpness of shape or sound is rare and thus intensely noticeable when it does occur.

Smells of mosses and musty mud rise from the ground as you enter the woods of Cwm Gwynon. Ferns and fungi too can be detected by their smell. The stream babbles and light twinkles on the water, bustling from rock to rock. The record of your walk is left on your face and hands: smooth fresh-water droplets, brushes

OPPOSITE Snow at Middleton – during the construction works, trees and habitats were fenced for protection.

with overhanging foliage, a gust of air, and if you're unlucky the sharp interruption of a bramble, thorn or nettle. All these small details fall away as you cross the woodland's edge into the open park. Wider views replace nature's minutiae. Now, the broad vision takes over and you have a fairly constant picture before you. There is Paxton's Tower, the Great Glasshouse, you're at Middleton and you move through the picture as it slowly changes – as if in a 'panning' sequence of shifting camera-angles. The place you are now in differs from the woods where each picture changed into another with almost every tree that you passed.

The quality of what you see is softened, regardless of the weather. In the scene I recall, it is softened by a haze of moisture, but even in bright sun, lush greens are everywhere. And when the grasses are parched and their flower-stalks bleached of chlorophyll, the trees and hedges still brush the view with their green tints to soften the scenery. Underfoot, too, softness shapes the landscape. The structure of the land has been gently moulded over millennia into undulations caused by ice and other geological processes.

The wood was soft and the green fields are too. But how different these two places are. According to Jay Appleton, originator of the 'Prospect-Refuge' theory of how we experience landscapes, these two contrasting places represent quintessential landscape types. We respond with equal delight, and in different ways, to places of refuge like the wood and to places of prospect

LEFT *The woodland edge —
light and shadow on a
winter evening.*

where we gain a commanding view over a wide area. This happens
at Middleton. The contrast is fundamental to the ways in which
we experience a place. Add to this the enrichment which we get
from the way we see, hear, smell and feel landscapes — sometimes
we can even taste them, especially in gardens. Now, we are
beginning to grasp what it means to acquire a 'sense of place'. Let
us think further about how we have experienced this place.

Beyond the five senses, 'the prevailing character' of a landscape
can be appreciated through the associations or suggestions which
it conjures in the mind. Memory comes in here, as Simon Schama's
televised book *Landscape and Memory* testifies. Places contain echoes
of their pasts, but the prevailing character derives primarily from
physical features. We measure the balance of its constituent parts
and register the presence or absence of dynamic movement. We
observe colour and texture. We seek out pictorial contrasts
between those two opposites on the prospect-refuge scale: 'empty'
and 'filled' space. Landscape artists use the device of foreground
or side-screen objects to frame a view, to enhance perspective and
otherwise to generate interest. Furthermore, we seem

subconsciously and naturally to evaluate the relationship between
the physical qualities within a place and those which lie just beyond
it. There are so many ingredients to the experience of landscape,
and we respond to them all. Alexander Pope famously employed
the word 'genius' to refer to a spirit that governs all the attributes
of a place and intercedes in our responses to it.

> *Consult the Genius of the Place in all;*
> *That tells theWaters or to rise, or fall,*
> *Or helps th'ambitious Hill the heav'ns to scale,*
> *Or scoops in circling theatres theVale;*
> *Calls in the Country, catches op'ning glades,*
> *Joins willing woods, and varies shades from shades . . .*

(FROM EPISTLE TO LORD BURLINGTON, 1728)

FORM,. COLOUR AND CONTRAST

Though he was advising a friend about the ideal method of laying
out ornamental grounds, Pope might have been writing the verse
above about Middleton itself! Water rises here in plenty and falls

OPPOSITE *The subtle
shades of late autumn on
the estate — from Llyn
Mawr, a lake which has yet
to be restored.*

in numerous places over ledges, weirs and cascades on its way to meet the river Tywi. There are 'ambitious' hills rising to the skyline. The slopes of the large natural bowl in which Middleton lies are 'scooped' with concavities. The lower ground has humps and hollows, and the bulk of the scattered woodlands provides shaggy frames that give shape to the intervening grassland. All around are different shades of green, constantly altering in the visual joy of Wales' changing light.

Colours can be named subtly here because there are at least three words for green in the Welsh language: *gwyrdd*, *glas* and *ir*. *Glas* means blue too, but also grey occasionally. For that colour there are the additional words *llwyd* and *llwydwyn*. White can be either *gwyn* or *can*, and brown is *gwinau*, *cochddu* or *brown*. *Cochddu* in fact means 'red-black'. We are in a land where the separateness of colours is not as fixed as elsewhere. Remember that these Celtic words have been current for some 2,500 years in Wales. Welsh has a greater range of words with which to describe colours and natural features than English, and invites us to discovery and response in the landscape.

What did Pope mean by 'varying shades from shades'? We have considered the shades of different hue, so that leaves the shady gloom that gives the woods their atmosphere. This shade varies too according to the size and type of the overarching trees. At dusk, the magic of Middleton is dynamised by the differences between the shade inside and outside the wood, and the way the darkness gathers differently on eastern, western, northern and southern-facing flanks of the bowl.

Perhaps the greatest strength of Middleton's setting by comparison with other botanic gardens, which are mainly urban rather than rural, is included in Pope's exhortation of the qualities of the 'genius' – it is the way it 'calls in the country'. In the park you are surrounded by rural Carmarthenshire. No matter how many come to this place, no matter how busy it may become, the Garden will always derive a distinctive spirit from the interplay between traditional 'country' and its monumental centrepiece – the Great Glasshouse. While the scale of the latter is majestic, the even grander scale of the former is only an infinitesimal part of the totality of Wales, and a far smaller element again of the landscape of Earth. Embedding the Great Glasshouse in an intricate pattern

of small fields, ancient hedgerows, larger blocks of woodland, and winding country lanes creates a sublime contrast.

If we think of the Middleton estate as occupying the bottom of a shallow bowl of land, the country that is 'called in' is represented by the sloping sides of that bowl. What of the territory beyond the brim? Paxton's Tower, and some high points in the area around the Great Glasshouse and on top of the Moorland Hill west of the Walled Garden, afford us distant views outwards. To the north, the southerly hills of the Cambrian mountains are discernible. From the Tower, the foreground is occupied by a plunging view into the valley where the Tywi river meanders in huge curves through lush meadows as it flows gently down towards Carmarthen in the west. Dryslwyn Castle stands proudly on a massive rock beside the river to the east, and Dinefwr Castle is a few miles further east.

The parallels between Middleton's landscape and Pope's precepts are not coincidental. Although it was not designed by Pope, Lord Burlington or 'Capability' Brown, Middleton's park and gardens were laid out in the final years of the 18th century. To its new owner, Middleton presented exciting landscape capabilities. By the time that Sir William Paxton was preparing for his return from Calcutta to Britain, the influence of British gardening had already crossed the English Channel demonstrating the extent to which the landscape phenomenon was securing a place for itself as a major category in the history of art. Rousseau had become an advocate of the 'natural' garden and G-L Le Rouge was publishing his *Cahiers* showing the disposition of places throughout Europe where *le jardin anglais* was the height of fashion. Paxton must consequently have been alert to the 'genius' of the place in his search for a country estate.

ABOVE *Dryslwyn Castle, with the river Tywi in the foreground.*

BELOW *The hoary silhouette of Dinefwr Castle, the home of Welsh kings until its capture by Edward I of England in the 1280s – a silent sentinel guarding the Tywi Valley at Llandeilo.*

NATURAL HISTORY

Middleton's sense of place is conditioned by two main histories: its natural history and its cultural history. Both of these provide the background knowledge which help us to enhance our primary visual appreciation of landscape. The natural history starts with the geology of the place, to which Jay Appleton refers in the next chapter. The events which formed the land before the advent of humans are fundamental, and they determined the nature of the soils on the estate. The story of Welsh geology is told by the rocks displayed, according to the order of their formation, along The Broadwalk as one enters the Garden. They are awe-inspiring and Gillian Clarke pays them a tribute in the poetry that she has written especially for this book.

Its indigenous natural history is the foundation of the Botanic Garden's living systems. Varied topography provides a wide range of microclimates and thus favours biodiversity, and opportunities for introducing all sorts of species with different requirements. There is a good quantity of established woodland including oaks, some of which are truly venerable, fine mature sweet chestnuts and other trees. The climate is wetter and warmer than in many other parts of Britain. Its greatest attribute, perhaps, is Middleton's shelter from the damaging effects of atmospheric pollution. Unless polluting industry develops down-wind, a westerly site like this benefits from the cleansing effects of the prevailing Atlantic winds, and the organisms which grow here are the first beneficiaries. The rain for which Wales is renowned has a special role too. In recent years, we have heard predictions of devastating droughts and global warming but, to the certain benefit of its botanical collections, Middleton should suffer less from these than the colder and drier eastern parts of the British Isles.

A detailed survey of the site's flora and fauna was made early in the project. Rare fungi and lichens thrive, indicating a plentiful supply of clean air and moisture. In 1990, I received a letter from Ray Woods of the Nature Conservancy Council confirming 'The valley woodland . . . supported *Prenula* and *Phaeographis* species [of lichens], which are associated with some of the purest air conditions in the country.' A further condition is important to the survival of certain vulnerable species: the absence of intensive farming for well over a century. Where major changes in land

management practices have not occurred, such as in historic parks, the biological diversity of lower plants and invertebrates is often found to be uncommonly rich. Middleton is a case in point.

Moisture collecting in the lowest parts of the landscape bowl has given rise to alder carr communities, particularly in the southern area. Marshy spots closer to the core of the Garden contain interesting and scarce wetland species, including marsh orchids, plume thistles and whorled caraway. During the landscaping works, areas of botanical interest such as these were protected as 'no-go' zones. Ferns are abundant: spleenworts, hart's-tongues, male and buckler-ferns, shield-ferns and hard-ferns, and polypodys all over the place on old trees and walls as well as on the ground.

ABOVE *Unfolding 'fiddleheads' of male fern,* Dryopteris filix-mas — *one of Britain's most common woodland ferns.*

The aquatic habitats are also abundant: there are at least four springs and watercourses on the site. Although the range of marginal plants is currently quite limited, there are ample opportunities for habitat restoration here. And there are the 18th-century lakes. All of them were defunct until the current project. Within the last two years, two have been restored as will the others when the substantial necessary funds are secured. The aquatic diversity of Middleton will flow from these sources.

HUMAN HISTORY

The history of Middleton prior to the coming of the nabob, Sir William Paxton, is sketchy. The land would have been taken into agriculture from the wild at an uncertain date. In the 17th century, the house belonged to the Middleton family. The Middletons may have had what we would understand as a small country estate, but the extent of any ornamental grounds is unknown. In the following century, it passed by marriage into the family of Gwyn, who held

it until William Paxton purchased it in 1789. Paxton used the wealth he had acquired in India to regenerate an estate that had suffered from the debts and mortgages of the last few generations of Gwyns.

The great architect of the country houses Sezincote and Daylesford in Gloucestershire, S P Cockerell, was engaged in 1793. Cockerell had just completed Daylesford for Warren Hastings, formerly Governor General in India. According to Henry Skrine, describing the new mansion in 1798, it 'far eclipses the proudest of the Cambrian mansions in Asiatic pomp and splendour; this house may justly be admired for the exterior beauty of its figure, as well as for its internal elegance. . .'. Paxton was an aesthete rich enough to undertake grand works. When he came to sell in 1824, having established public baths at Tenby and a water supply for Carmarthen, and having stood as a member of parliament, the sale catalogue revealed embellishments such as a pheasantry, and a 'lofty plantation of firs' screening 'a handsome

THE ICE-HOUSE

Door into the hill.
Bat hibernarium.
Echo-box.

Not frigidaire.
Not our immaculate tabernacles
of white enamel,

but house of zipping shadows,
a winter harvest packed
as tight as bales.

*

With axe, saw, grappling iron, block and tackle,
they'd lift the lid off the lake.
In a rare year an acre
could yield a thousand tons.

Then heavy horses hauled it up the hill
to stack those blocks of luminous blue,
sky turned to glass, each one clear
to the needle of light at its core.

In a bad year when the lakes didn't freeze
they'd take ponies to the mountain,
unlock ravines of snow, or sever
the tangled locks of a waterfall.

*

A lemon bloomed with frost,
hollowed and filled with sweet snow.
A bowl of ice and Muscat grapes.
A misted glass of wine.

Did Paxton know these things, and bring from India
his dreams of ice and water engineering?
Or from the Mughal gardens his design
of cool reflections and the sound of water?

From his Tower he'd see it all: a garden of streams,
sluices, dams, cascades, and a house on a hill
in a chain of lakes, with reservoirs and ice-ponds,
the healing waters of chalybeate springs.

He took water to his gate for public use,
to save the rural poor from the scourge of filth
and fevers, devised, a hundred years ahead
of his time, a water system for Carmarthen.

In cisterns, pipes, drains, faucets, closets,
water flowed through his house. Above the springs
with their medicinal powers, he built a bath-house
in a flower garden, that they might take the waters,

and flower-scents, steam and iron minerals
bring the colour to dear Maria's cheek
and cool the fevers of childhood, as they basked
in the opulence of water.

*

A banquet in the vale of Tywi. Guests
from London. His house complete, long windows
flame with candle-light. Bat-shadows
scribble on the dusk, the house reflects
in its ring of lakes. Music. Murmurs of silk.
Perhaps they sip from goblets made of ice,
admire the fountain table centrepiece,
a swan floating on snow and sweet milk,
and trapped in an obelisk of glass, live fish
flicker. Piled in their frozen pyramids,
ice-apples, peaches, apricots, mulberries, figs,
among glowing jellies, junkets, creams, a dish
of fine rose-scented butter. Such a stir
it must have caused in deep Carmarthenshire.

Gillian Clarke

conservatory about thirty-six feet long, stored with productive vines; a flower garden round and lawn in front with dry gravelled walks, and folding gates at the entrance; walks through the plantation to a capital kitchen garden, walled round and clothed with choice well-selected fruit trees, stocked, cropped and planted, containing about three acres; capital hot-house, peachery and grape house, &c.'.

The description continues, 'a good orchard, well planted with young trees; an ice house, etc. Melon ground, pine pits, &c.'. Gravelled walks branched in various directions through the park. Some led to 'a beautiful lake of fine clear water, of considerable extent'. A succession of views delighted the visitor together with 'an enchanting dell, with a flower garden: a rustic building, with a chalybeate, and vapour bath, with dressing rooms, &c.'. There was a grotto and a further chalybeate spring, seemingly piped from the lake! The description praised the exquisite taste of Paxton's park 'richly ornamented by nature, and greatly improved by art' and drew special attention to the various water works including hot and cold bath houses and 'a majestic waterfall, enlivened by flower gardens, and the interesting scenery that alternately presents itself to the eye'. The views of the vale of Tywi, Dinefwr Castle, the ruins of Dryslwyn Castle, and the Grongar Hills were noted, and the patriotic Gothic tower, erected by Paxton in memory of Lord Nelson, was described as a 'grand ornament and landmark in the county', as it remains to this day.

The design of Middleton's park appears to have been the work of three men. A letter from Paxton to a friend records that Samuel Lapidge, a collaborator of Cockerell's and successor to Capability Brown's practice, laid out the lawn on which the Great Glasshouse now stands. S P Cockerell, the architect of Middleton Hall whose drawing of a small garden for Daylesford survives at the Royal Institute of British Architects, probably had a hand in the works too. Paxton's estate manager, a qualified engineer named James Grier, was remembered in his obituary notice for his 'peculiarly ingenious application of the theodolite'. Grier served Paxton for many years, firmly in control of estate improvements. The problem is that we do not know exactly who did what. Conceivably, others joined forces with Paxton in the great landscape project, which must have gone on for years.

I often wonder whose idea the lakes were. Paxton would certainly have wanted them, his life in Britain seems to have been devoted to water. It was William Emes who had the greatest reputation for making lakes in parks after the death of Capability Brown in 1783. He produced plans for Baron Hill, on Anglesey, Gregynog, Chirk and Powis Castles, and Penrice, which is not far from Middleton. One of his 'signatures' was a lake that tapered off obliquely into a narrow canal. This is just what the largest of Middleton's original four lakes does before discharging into the 'majestic waterfall' described by the 1824 Sales Particulars. There is no proof of Emes' involvement, but it is a tempting possibility, as he was one of the most successful landscape gardeners in the 1780s and 1790s after the death of Brown.

After 1824, the estate passed into the Adams family, who appear to have maintained Paxton's landscape concept largely unaltered. Their family fortunes waned and the last Adams left Middleton in the early years of the 20th century. The house, empty and silent, began to fall into disrepair. The grounds and lakes were untended. In 1931, the estate passed into the ownership of Carmarthenshire County Council. Shortly after, on 10 November of that year, the house burnt to the ground.

Middleton's fortunes have waxed and waned, but it has triumphed in adversity. The triumph shows through in the landscape. New chapters in the natural and human histories have started. A new layer is being added to the riches of the genius of the estate. The Middleton project seeks to tune the place more closely to nature and our ideas about nature's value. To quote from a recent essay by Jay Appleton 'Nature can indeed communicate her own narrative if we will let her. Perhaps we should make more of an effort to learn her language.' That must be a language that the new Botanic Garden can help us to understand.

Francis Bacon, writing in 1625, reminded us that 'God Almightie first Planted a Garden'. Ever since the days of Eden, gardens have encompassed and reflected problematic relationships but have also provided images of solace and salvation. They neatly circumscribe the interface between nature and human nature. The Garden at Middleton is now a place of transfer between human and other biologies – a place where knowledge will be both applied and gained. The histories continue and the genius lives on.

THE GARDEN AND THE WELSH LANDSCAPE

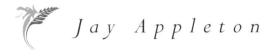

Jay Appleton

Imagine yourself standing on the slope of a mountain covered with forest, out of which have been cut a number of small clearances now filled with displays of plants. The white trunks of the gum trees and the brown fibrous textures of the stringy barks tell you unmistakably that you are somewhere in Australia. Through the occasional gaps in the trees you catch glimpses of distant objects, the ANZAC (Australian and New Zealand Army Corps) Memorial, the Federal Parliament House, the Government Offices and the looping shorelines of the great artificial lake which bears the name of Burley Griffin, architect of the Master Plan of Canberra, the city which, behind the screen of trees, lies at your feet.

THE AUSTRALIAN MODEL

Whatever we understand by the term 'national botanic garden', the Australian version has got to be, symbolically, the nearest approach to the ideal model. Plants from every part of the world are here, growing in conditions which, where necessary, have been made to approximate as closely as possible to those of their natural habitats, but they are all framed by the surrounding native trees, part of the primeval forest of that part of Australia. Their surround positively exudes the mood of the country, its natural symbolism reinforced by the cultural symbolism of those more distant icons of nationhood. The function of the garden in

presenting horticultural, botanical and ecological phenomena from anywhere in the world is not compromised by this combination of national and natural symbols. Standing as it does between nature and culture, the garden expresses the dual role of both in creating the landscape.

OPPOSITE *The Great Glasshouse in its landscape. Note the diversity of vegetation and blending of a huge artificial structure into the world of nature.*

RIGHT *The gum tree is typical of Australia – the buds and fruit of* Eucalyptus camaldulensis.

or not they are in flower, the spacing between them, and particularly the background. Painters make a conventional division of a landscape into foreground, middle ground and distance. If the primary object of our interest is in the foreground, we cannot mentally exclude the other two from our view, and we need to ask ourselves how, if at all, the wider landscape may be able to communicate a sense of 'Welshness' analogous to that Australian symbolism which permeates the gardens in Canberra. And it goes without saying that what applies to a plant in a herbaceous border applies equally to any artwork introduced into the garden. Thought must be given to its relationship with the whole picture of the landscape, not just its immediate surroundings.

LEFT AND BELOW
Eucalyptus trees provide the symbolic background for the Australian National Botanic Gardens, Canberra.

OPPOSITE *The Great Glasshouse, reflected in the still water, models the rounded hills typical of central South Wales.*

The natural vegetation of the Tywi Valley in which the National Botanic Garden of Wales is situated was cut down centuries ago, so obviously we cannot look directly to Canberra for a blueprint to use in Wales. We can, however, give the same serious consideration to the problem of presenting growing plants for the public to see, to understand and to enjoy, in a context which enhances the claim that this is more than just another garden that happens to be in Wales. How, in these very different circumstances, can it be uniquely 'Welsh'?

Perhaps we could usefully begin by reminding ourselves that, whenever we look at an object, the way we react to it is affected by everything within our field of vision. This is well understood by the designer of any art gallery. The framing of the pictures, the colour and texture of the walls, of the floor and of the ceiling, the spacing of the exhibits, the angle and intensity of the lighting – these have all to be determined after careful thought, since they can profoundly affect the way we interact with the exhibits.

By the same token, our perception of a plant growing in, say, a herbaceous border is subject to a whole range of comparable contextual influences – the colour of the adjacent plants, whether

THE WELSH LANDSCAPE

What, then, is the Welsh landscape? There is no single version of it. No individual garden can 'represent' Milford Haven, the Rhondda Valley, Snowdon, Blaenau Ffestiniog and the low, windswept plateau of Anglesey any more than Canberra could 'represent' the Hamersley Range, the Red Centre and the Snowy Mountains. What we are looking for is something, even if we cannot precisely define what it is, which somehow captures the mood of Wales.

The popular image of the Welsh landscape is based on the mountains and lakes of Snowdonia, and it might well be argued that a national garden could better capture the spirit of Wales if it were in the north rather than the south of the Principality. The fashion for the 'Picturesque' led tourists to Wales in the 1790s, but earlier than that a fascination with the wilder manifestations of nature had begun to grab the imagination of the public, and it continued as a criterion of beauty in landscape through the Romantic Period and, in some ways, up to our own time.

The basis of all landscape, the stage or platform on which it is set, is to be found in its geology, and our understanding of it requires at least a superficial familiarity with how its physical components originated. A glance at the geological map of the Ordnance Survey shows that the greater part of the grounds of Middleton Hall, including the site of the Hall itself, stands on Downtonian marls at the base of the Old Red Sandstone, but that, almost immediately to the north of the Hall, one passes on to a narrow outcrop of the Silurian, (the Ludlow and Wenlock Series), and then almost immediately, across an unconformity, on to the Ordovician. These two systems, the Ordovician and the Silurian, occupy most of Central Wales, reaching as far as the North Wales coast, as well as the gentler undulating surfaces of the Tywi Valley between Llandeilo and Carmarthen.

The major divisions of the geological map, however, are based on the age of the deposits rather than their rock types. If we look more closely we shall find that, in the northern Ordovician, unlike in the Tywi Valley, the sedimentary rocks (sandstones, limestones, shales etc.) are frequently mixed with rocks of igneous origin. These igneous rocks, being much harder, have introduced an altogether rougher aspect which is partly

THE ARTIST'S LANDSCAPE

BELOW *A painting of Cader Idris by Richard Wilson. A combination of igneous rocks and glaciated landforms makes for dramatic landscapes in parts of North Wales.*

Writers like William Gilpin, an account of whose tour of North Wales in 1773, '*relative chiefly to natural beauty*', was published in 1809, and George Borrow, whose *Wild Wales* appeared in 1862, caught the imagination of early British tourists, and consolidated the image of Wales in Snowdonia terms. Most of the great landscape painters tried their hands on Cader Idris or the lakes of North Wales. The prominence of Snowdonia as a subject for painters was demonstrated by Peter Howard's research, published in 1991. He noted the locations of the subjects of all the landscape paintings exhibited at the Royal Academy of Arts in London between 1769 and 1980. In each of six periods within this time span, Snowdonia remained the most popular Welsh subject for the landscape painter, though the Tywi Valley was by no means neglected, especially in the earlier years.

responsible for giving Snowdonia its more dramatic landforms and Wales most of its highest mountains, including Snowdon, the Glyders, the Carneddau, Cader Idris, Aran Mawddwy, Arenig Fawr and Arenig Fach.

Add to this the effect of glaciation, which in the higher elevations of North Wales produced many spectacular landforms like corries (little basin-like features backed by steep screes or even precipices, and usually containing small tarns), arêtes (those knife-edged ridges which provide such dramatic skylines), waterfalls and, of course, the lakes themselves. Further south, although the Tywi Valley was occupied by a glacier, the elevations were not high enough to produce these dramatic effects, and glacial activity consisted mainly of the deposition of boulder clay and other deposits, as on the flanks of the little valley containing the lakes at Middleton, which had the effect of smoothing out rather than sharpening up the configurations of the landscape.

We can see, therefore, why the decision to locate the National Botanic Garden in the south rather than the north might provoke some people to question whether it was in the right place. But the choice of Middleton Hall out of a number of potential sites was based on a wide range of criteria, some of which were properly accorded more importance than the dominance of the Snowdonian image as the accepted symbol of the Welsh landscape. Physical conditions, for example, ruled out many sites. The high rainfall in Snowdonia could well present problems for the growing of plants from drier climates, at least out of doors. Given an adequate supply of water, it is easier to remedy a deficiency of rainfall in dry areas than to create drought conditions in wet ones. In an ordinary ornamental garden this might not matter, because one would be free to choose plant materials suited to the wetter climate; but in a national botanic garden one has to be able to accommodate species whose inclusion is determined by other criteria, and a site which could not grow them would clearly be unacceptable.

The question before us at the moment, then, is not whether Middleton was the 'best' of the available sites, but how it fits into the Welsh landscape, and, far as they may be from the authentic Snowdonian image, these gentler glaciated scarplands of the Tywi Valley, though less dramatic, are typical of much larger areas of Wales than is the wilder scenery of Gwynedd.

DEVONIAN

Old Red Sandstone.
The rose-red fields of Brecon.
The first leaf, first sign of land,
when Wales was a fragment of Pangaea,
marooned in that mighty continent
till, driven by the heartbeat of the earth,
it broke into drifting lands
and the oceans found their names.

Gillian Clarke

The phrase 'the Welsh landscape' conjures up a picture of a phenomenon which not only varies strikingly from place to place but has also been subject to two kinds of change. First, it has changed physically, being the product of evolution on a geological, and more recently, a much shorter timescale. Following the clearance of the forests, new patterns have evolved as a result of economic activities. These are mainly associated with agriculture, but, in some areas, with mining, quarrying, manufacturing and other industries. Latterly re-afforestation has had a profound effect on the uplands, but certainly it is agriculture which has been the most influential agent of change over Wales as a whole, so the view of the surrounding landscape from Middleton Hall would, in this sense, be as typical as any site one could find.

THE PERCEPTION OF LANDSCAPE AND THE ROLE OF THE IMAGINATION

The word 'landscape' implies the environment visually perceived, and the second kind of change concerns the ways in which we see it. Attitudes towards re-afforestation, for example, have always been ambivalent. Wordsworth said of the larch that it was 'less than any other pleasing' and that 'its green is so peculiar and vivid, that, finding nothing to harmonise with it, wherever it comes forth, a disagreeable speck is produced'. It is (in summer) 'of dingy lifeless hue', (in autumn) 'of a spiritless unvaried yellow' and (in winter) it 'appears absolutely dead'. He strongly resented its intrusion into the landscape, yet today it is regarded by many with nostalgic affection as an essential icon of the Lake District.

An even more controversial element in the landscape is water. The rivers, waterfalls and glacial lakes of Wales are universally admired, but the construction of artificial reservoirs in Wales has almost always met with vociferous protest. Nevertheless, if you go to Lake Vyrnwy or the Elan Valley today you will encounter coach parties of tourists who have often travelled long distances to admire them. Improbable as it may now seem, even oilseed rape could eventually draw admiring crowds!

Our habits of perception are the products of the sum of our individual experiences working on what we have inherited genetically. We see the landscape through what the American philosopher, George Kelly, calls a 'templet' – a constantly changing screen, unique to each of us as individuals, which filters out some things, accentuates others and endows the objects which make up the landscape and their arrangements with a significance peculiarly our own. Often we can recognise habits of perception

which are characteristic of whole categories or sub-categories of communities, but we must always allow that, within any group of visitors to the Garden, there will always be a range of people with different interests, different levels of understanding and expertise, different ways of interacting with what the Garden can offer. People brought up in a Welsh culture, for example, may well read messages into the landscape which the English could miss. The Welsh language is exceptionally rich in words descriptive of topographical features, and a high proportion of Welsh place names consist simply of the compounding of such words. To a Welsh person merely to pronounce such a place name is to call up a visual image of it. A wide divergence of visitor response, then, is the first of two challenges the Garden has to meet.

The second challenge arises from the fact that no botanic garden, any more than a museum, can display more than a tiny fraction of the material which could legitimately be regarded as relevant to its purpose. One criterion of its success is its capacity for stimulating the imagination into exploring those connections which relate the objects displayed to the various contexts which give them meaning. If we visit an art gallery and find there a single example of the work of Rembrandt, it is to be hoped that we shall find ourselves asking questions not just about the other works of this one painter, but about those of his contemporaries, about the influence of his predecessors on his style, his brushwork, his use

RIGHT *Lake Vyrnwy, Powys. Note the juxtaposition of trees and water against the background of low hills.*

of pigments, his application of the rules of perspective, and so on.
Each of these questions can spark off a line of enquiry which, if
pursued, will extend our understanding of a much wider field of
experience than is contained within the exhibit or, indeed, the
gallery, but the key to this whole process is the imagination. The
exhibit itself is the trigger which fires off a kind of chain reaction
of investigative events.

THE GARDEN IN THE LANDSCAPE

If we apply this approach to the botanic garden, we can see the
importance of maximising the opportunities for sparking off chain
reactions of this sort. By labelling plants with their Latin names,
for example, we can place them in a taxonomic context which
links them to other groups of plants to which they are botanically
related. By the use of diagrams we can explain how the various
parts of a plant, which we can see, collectively discharge the

functions which enable it to remain alive and to reproduce its species, even though we may not be able to see these processes actually taking place.

In the same way, by the use of appropriate maps, we can indicate the world distribution of the plants we are looking at and steer the imagination towards the understanding of that phenomenon, which mostly lies far, far beyond the limits of visibility. The field of relevance stretches from the poles to the equator, from the Tywi Valley to that little outpost of Welsh culture in the Chubut Valley of Patagonia. Yet the first link in that chain, which eventually encompasses the earth, is the Garden itself and that little fragment of the Welsh landscape which immediately surrounds it, which is incorporated in the visual image of the Garden, and which can discharge a symbolic role in helping us to find our own most meaningful interpretation of what the National Botanic Garden of Wales signifies to each one of us.

In helping the visitor to make this symbolic connection between the Garden and the wider landscape the design team has contrived some imaginative devices. For example, the little 'rill', which conveys a serpentine trickle of water down The Broadwalk, can be seen as mimicking the meanders of the river Tywi. The dome of the Great Glasshouse models the rounded shapes of the surrounding hills, one of which, Grongar, just across the Tywi, was the subject of one of the earliest purely descriptive landscape poems in the English language. The huge imported rocks of different geological ages along The Broadwalk are reminders of the stratigraphical sequence of the material of which the country of Wales is built.

Seen from the higher ground in the Garden, the perimeter fence is overtopped on nearly every side by the landscape of grassland farming, by far the most common type of agricultural landscape in Wales. There is scarcely an arable field in sight, so the colour scheme is entirely dominated by green, criss-crossed by the variable shades of the hedgerows and punctuated by small copses and scattered trees. Where the bare earth does manage to show through, the green is offset by its complementary colour, red, which might even suggest to a sensitive patriot the colours of the Welsh dragon as depicted on the official emblem of the Garden!

Since the estate contains more land than is required for horticultural purposes, parts of it towards the margins are being left in agricultural use, and this will allow the surrounding grassland to spill over the boundary fence, as it were, thus providing yet another visual link between the Garden and the landscape beyond. On the south, east and west the horizon rises higher than the Garden, but on the northern side a high ridge, which, to the north-east supports the eye-catching folly of Paxton's Tower, is broken by the valley of the little Afon Gwynon as it makes its exit from the Garden to join the river Tywi, thus opening up a much longer view deep into Central Wales.

MIDDLETON – THE IDEAL SETTING

Middleton Hall, then, as a setting for the National Botanic Garden, is admirably endowed with environmental advantages. What the Canberra site demanded was a visual reminder of the character of a young country, only a small proportion of which had so far had its natural aspect radically altered by the cultural impact of its human occupants. This function was and is perfectly discharged by the matrix of native 'bush' into which it has been accommodated. What its Welsh counterpart demanded as a backcloth was something quite different: a landscape which somehow symbolised an evolutionary process. In this evolutionary process, eons of geological history had been succeeded by a relatively short but intensive period of human intervention that radically altered the appearance of the landscape through centuries of agricultural activity, punctuated by occasional attempts to create landscapes as works of art.

Viewed from the Garden itself, the undulating terrain rises from the little valley of the Gwynon, with its chain of ornamental lakes, and is endowed with numerous vantage points. This turns a mere site into a 'landscape' in something like the tradition of 'The Picturesque', which dictated the fashionable style when the park was laid out two hundred years ago. Beyond, on every side, lies the Welsh countryside, the product of hundreds of years of farming, but which still owes its major relief features to hundreds of millions of years of a rich geological history. Any visitor who can bring an equally rich imagination to match the legacy of nature, of culture, and of the ingenuity of the Garden's design team can hardly fail to find their imagination well rewarded.

OPPOSITE *'Blending into the landscape'. The garden has been re-created out of the 'Picturesque' landscape designed two centuries ago.*

THE NATURE AND CULTURE OF PLANTS IN WALES

James Robertson

It is a common assumption that nature comprises all that is natural, but excludes humans. Culture is a uniquely human attribute, the result of human communities straining towards perfection. Between them lies an unbridgeable divide.

But an examination of the relationship between wild plants and people in Wales dispels such easy divisions. The natural vegetation of Wales has played its part in shaping human culture, and has adapted successfully to it in the past. The links between the two run deep. It is apt that Wales should have a botanic garden not only to celebrate its wild plants, but also to bridge the gulf between culture and nature.

At one time the term 'culture' embraced the practice of growing and tending plants in gardens. When this 'culture' later became known as horticulture, it took a step away from the centre of human life. Plants then became objects of manipulation by an increasingly sophisticated science, rather than the occupants of the land on which humans and their animals depended. Through dissection and analysis, science has given us knowledge, but not necessarily understanding. The challenge for science in the new millennium is one of synthesis rather than analysis. We need to draw together what we know about ourselves and the natural world if we are to manage ourselves, and in turn manage the global economy and ecology in a sustainable manner.

The beginnings of a synthesis of knowledge can be found in the field of medicine. The shortcomings of too specialised an approach to medicine are opening up an appreciation of the ecology of the human body – it is better to treat the whole body than to address only individual symptoms. Many alternative approaches towards human health have emerged, one consequence of which has been a heightened interest in traditional herbal medicines.

THE HERBALIST TRADITION

Herbalism has a noble tradition in Wales. Although early written accounts of remedies are sparse, at least some of the profusion of folk remedies which existed as an integral part of rural life are still with us. Research I carried out for the book *Flora Britannica* unlocked many childhood memories of the medicinal use of wild plants. This selection gives an indication of how important a resource wild plants were, and how much knowledge people had about them.

Bog bean was collected and boiled up to make a tea for the treatment of 'rheumatics'. Male fern was used for the treatment of tapeworm, acting as a knock-out drop so that the parasite loosened its intestinal grip and could be expelled from the body. Buckthorn, as well as providing a green and yellow dye from its berries, yielded a purgative from its bark. Sweet flag rhizomes were dried and used as an aromatic stimulant. White and black horehound were used as cough mixtures. Horseradish and celery

OPPOSITE *Marsh mallow was the first plant to be recorded from Wales, but it is now extinct; its starchy roots were used to make sweets.*

were eaten, as part of a meat-free diet, to treat rheumatism, gout and arthritis. Bistort leaves were used by children to line their shoes to ease aching feet. Stonecrop was simmered in lard and mixed with flowers of sulphur to treat shingles.

Most plants now used in herbal remedies are grown for the purpose. The raw materials which wild plants once provided are now supplied by crops, whether of timber, or hemp for rope making, or rye grass for fodder. We should not forget that plants have evolved their infinite variety and potency through the mediation of animals, whether herbivores or pollinators. Humans are part of that evolutionary adventure.

In the past, when people were more closely connected to the land, wild plants played a practical role in the lives of rural communities. They were the stuff of survival. As well as the source of medicines, they provided food, fodder, fertiliser, fuel and raw materials.

BELOW *The acrid* Sedum *or biting stonecrop, which gets its name form the sharply bitter taste of its leaves, has been used in the treatment of shingles.*

ABOVE *A tea was once brewed from the trifoliate leaves of bog bean, which look very like those of a water-loving broad bean, and taken as a cure for 'rheumatics'.*

THE PHYSICIANS OF MYDDFAI

Herbalism was one of the rural arts being practised by the men of knowledge, or 'Gwyddoniaid', before 1000 BC. It had developed into a tested way of treating diagnosed symptoms with carefully prepared medicines by the time of the Physicians of Myddfai. The first Physicians were three brothers born of the union between the legendary 'Lady of the Lake' from nearby Llyn y Fan Fach, and a local farmer. Their medical knowledge was bequeathed to posterity through manuscripts dating from the 13th century.

The legendary medical skills of this dynasty of doctors reflect the advances in medicine made between the 9th and 15th centuries. Their reputed magical powers were based on a good understanding of the local flora, and the attributes of different wild plants.

RIGHT *Snowdrops growing in the graveyard of the medieval Church of St Michael, Myddfai.*

FAR RIGHT *The 18th-century tombstone of David and John Jones, surgeons of Myddfai descended from the Physicians.*

THE PHYSICIANS OF MYDDFAI

1 LLYN Y FAN FACH

Like a bowl of milk
the mountain cups the lake
deep and dark as the past,
and history's lost
where the Ages of Stone,
Bronze and Iron left their bones
under the earth, under the water
with the lake king's daughter.

Look into that surface.
It's not your face
you see, but hers,
as the wind stirs
water's mirror.
Wind turns the pages of the book
of history, each leaf
not yours but a people's grief.

2 THREE CHANCES

The ages drown, dissolved into the past,
the stories of the island lie half lost
in legend and archaeology, in the myths
and silts of ancient settlements.

With his mother's bread he won her from
    the lake,
three loaves, three chances for love to break
the boundaries of earth and water, to crack
time and the elements.

Three strikes of metal and she was gone.
Three sons, they say, were born of that union
of Stone Age and Celt, of stone and iron,
of earth-skills and art.

Their inheritance their father's grief,
their mother's way with herbs, with root
    and leaf,
the distillations of plants to bring relief
to body and heart.

3 THE HEALERS OF MYDDFAI

Linctus, cordials, electuaries, quoils,
conserves of borage, bugloss and burdock,
scurvy grass, cowslip, wormwood, rue.

The sons of the sons of the sons
of the woman of water
and the man of the earth,
carried the art of healing
down the generations,
as if the human mind
were an amphora of precious oils
that must never be spilt.

Bittersweet, dove's foot, nailwort,
    thorough wax,
hemlock, tamarisk, colt's foot, thornberry,
heartsease, honeysuckle, calamint,
    camomile.

History's blurred with legend,
but the physicians' names
are on the graves at Myddfai,
their secrets buried with their bones.
This garden's a safe house
for wild and tame. The otter's home,
black oil sleeking the night river
leaving its sprent on the stones.

Snakeweed, angelica, periwinkle, balm,
adders tongue, betony, bugle, burnet,
crowsfoot, henbane, watercress, sorrel.

From them we might have learned
the healing balm of plants.
Will this be the day they loose
the furious gene, trampling
the heal-all that grows secretly
in a field singing with bees,
that might have given us what science
seeks in its test-tubes and trays?

Tormentil, woundwort, plantain, dock,
comfrey, horsetail, briony, scabious,
hyssop, mallow, mustard, mint.

Gillian Clarke

RAW MATERIALS FOR SURVIVAL

Plants have a place in traditional Welsh cuisine. Two species of seaweed, sea lettuce and *laver* or *llawr* in Welsh, have long been used for soups and purées, the latter known as laverbread. The seaweed was gathered and cured in great stacks on the Pembrokeshire coast, and it is harvested still. Plants used in cooking, brewing and conserves include elderflower and elderberry, blackberry, haws (for a Turkish delight-type sweet), wild garlic, sorrel, sea kale, sloes and nettles. In addition, various herbs are used as flavourings and garnishes.

BELOW *A photograph of Newborough ladies at work making traditional marram grass products on Newborough Dunes, Anglesey, a century ago.*

RIGHT *Young shoots of sea kale have long been enjoyed as a delicacy; wild plants suffered from unscrupulous harvesting by the Victorians.*

RIGHT *Aromatic elderflowers offer culinary delights, while the bush is said to have awesome magical powers.*

BELOW *Wild garlic is often abundant in wet woods. Its leaves can be chopped and sprinkled onto salads or used to flavour casseroles and stews.*

People can no longer rely on the abundant plants of field and hedgerow to enliven dishes; anyway, alternatives are readily available in the supermarket. But some wild plants are still in common culinary use: elderflowers are picked to make champagne and fritters, wild blackberries have not been entirely displaced by pick-your-own cultivars for puddings and conserves, and nettle soup has become a stand-by for new ruralists.

The economy of rural Wales is still predominantly pastoral, and this has determined the way that communities lived in the past. Farms and smallholdings were scattered, but each depended on its neighbour. Indeed, much of the land was shared as commons and mountain grazings. The area of common land in Wales today is much reduced, but still approaches 200,000 hectares, or 10% of the total land area.

The rocky terrain, which defied the plough, and the way in which the land was farmed, meant that rural communities depended on the natural vegetation to feed their stock. They modified it, for example by burning upland heaths to produce a flush of grass and more palatable young heather, but they did not destroy it and replace it with rye grass monocultures.

Seaweed was harvested to fertilise fields within horse and cart distance of the coast. Supplemented by ancient plant material in the form of coal, fuel came from self-sustaining native peatlands and woodlands. The cutting and stacking of peat was a characteristic feature of rural life in parts of Wales into the 1900s. Woodlands were managed for a range of products: doors, windows, floors and roofing timbers for houses, and also wattle chimneys, which were made from hazel; farm equipment, such as milk pails, butter churns and farm tools; fences and hurdles to pen stock; and so on.

There was a thriving marram-weaving industry in the 19th century, located on Wales' once-extensive sand dune systems, such as those along the southwest coast of Anglesey. Marram grass was used to make mats for haystacks; for barn roofs and cucumber frames; for nets and cordage for fishermen; and grass ropes for packing. Even shoes were woven out of marram. The tall grass was cut in late summer with a broad-bladed reaping hook, heaped and spread to dry in sheltered dune slacks. By tradition, each family had its own sand dune. Harvesting alone took a month, with most of the community engaged in the industry.

Bracken was commonly cut for bedding for livestock in winter. Gorse mills were widespread, crushing gorse to overcome its spiny unpalatability and provide a valuable fodder for horses. Heather was used in packaging, to stop breakages of bricks being exported to Ireland, at a time when straw was forbidden because of the risk of foot and mouth disease.

Wild plants performed a myriad of other functions. They were indicators of mineral deposits: early mineralogists seeking copper had to be good botanists. Forked spleenwort and alpine pennycress are now more or less confined to the spoil heaps which are all that remain of the lead mines which they may have once revealed. Rare plants and ferns were sought after by Victorian plants collectors, spawning a cottage industry of 'mountain guides' and plant-hunters, and plants stimulated nearly 500 years of botany in Wales.

WELSH BOTANY

Although local people were probably already aware of the plants of their neighbourhood, the first written references to Welsh plants were in the manuscript of a herbal attributed to William Salusbury (1520–84). The localities of ten plants near Denbigh were listed, and the first plant mentioned was the marsh mallow *Althaea officinalis* (Hocys y Morfa in Welsh). Sugar and starch-rich roots were used to make a sweet, and are still used to placate teething infants, although the modern sweet of the same name no longer has any connection with the plant. Tellingly, it is now extinct in Wales.

The first published records of Welsh plants were in the second edition of Gerarde's *Herball*, with a number of records contributed by the Welshman Thomas Glynne from Glynllifon. The *Herball* included three plants from Wales new to Britain, mountain sorrel, moss campion and alpine saxifrage.

In the British context it was the mountain flora of Wales which figured prominently in early accounts. Edward Llwyd (1660–1707) contributed nearly fifty new records to John Ray's published plant records, including the Snowdon Lily, most of which he discovered in the uplands of Wales. The foremost Welsh naturalists' society, Cymdeithas Edward Llwyd, takes its name from this eminent botanist.

Since Edward Llwyd's plant hunting days in the mountains of North Wales, a great number of professional and amateur botanists have contributed to the collection and classification of plant material, and the compilation of plant records by geographical area or vice-county. Many distinguished botanists operate in Wales today, whose knowledge should enrich the National Botanic Garden of Wales.

Modern botany, through the analysis of pollen and meticulous recording of plant distribution, reveals much about the nature of Wales, past and present, and helps guide the future actions of those working for the conservation of nature. Published accounts of the flora of Wales, such as county floras, add meaning and urgency to the task of conserving wild plants. The variety of natural habitats and the abundance and exuberance of Welsh plant life make this a wonderful country for plants and plant-hunters alike.

WHAT IS SPECIAL ABOUT THE PLANTS OF WALES?

With nearly one fifth of Britain's coastline, about 1,200 kilometres, Wales is framed by the sea, which profoundly influences its flora. The Oceanic climate and the influence of the Gulf Stream mean that low-lying, coastal districts can be almost frost free in winter. The prevailing southwesterly winds bring in weather fronts, and as the rain-charged air is forced to rise over high ground, it sheds its rain. The mountains which stretch from Snowdonia in the north through the spine of the Cambrian mountains, to the Brecon Beacons in the south, ensure that Wales is a land of lakes and rivers and water.

BELOW *Moss campion grows on mountain cliffs; its first British record was from Snowdonia.*

Snowdon is not only the highest mountain in England and Wales, at 1,085 metres; it is also the wettest place in Britain and Ireland, with annual rainfall averaging 4,500 millimetres. There are 15 high peaks in northwest Wales, 4 of which exceed 1,000 metres. But even in South Wales there are mountains; Pen y Fan in the Brecon Beacons, at 886 metres, is the highest Old Red Sandstone peak in Britain. Other superlatives include the highest waterfall in England and Wales, at Pistyll Rhaeadr in Clwyd; and the highest sand dune in Britain, at Merthyr Mawr, in Mid Glamorgan.

A small country with such varied geology lured many pioneers to Wales to study the subject and establish important geological principles from the rocks which they found. Two geological periods, the Ordovician and Silurian, are named after ancient Welsh tribes. Melting glaciers left their marks on Snowdonia a mere ten thousand years ago, making Snowdon one of the best places to study recent geological history.

This glacial history, geology and mountainous terrain, coupled with the climate and rainfall, all find expression in the plants which occur in Wales. The mild climate, clean air, rocks and water produce conditions ideally suited to those quintessentially Welsh

plants, the filmy ferns, mosses and lichens. They cling to rocks bathed in the fine plume of mist which rises from waterfalls, or adorn stunted trees in the sessile oak woods which clothe steep ridges. Three-quarters of all British moss and liverwort species are found in Wales, in humid ravines and on montane crags and screes, as well as in woods and on dunes. With well over a 1,000 species of lichen, the flora of Wales includes 8% of all lichen species known worldwide.

In an area of only 2,000 square kilometres, there are also over 1,000 species of flowering plants. This represents more than two-thirds of the British flora. It includes arctic-alpine plants at the southern edge of their range. Tufted saxifrage, for example, was stranded on craggy mountain tops in Snowdonia after the departure of the ice, where it is accompanied by the Snowdon Lily, at its only station in Britain. There are also warmth-loving flowers at their northernmost localities, and a group of oceanic rarities which have toeholds along Wales' magnificent coastline, but are otherwise restricted to Brittany and Ireland. These include hairy greenweed, prostrate asparagus, toadflax-leaved St John's wort, fen orchid, dune helleborine and spotted rockrose.

Some continental species find a home for themselves on the thin, dry soils of Denbighshire, located to the east of Snowdon, which captures most of the moisture from the prevailing westerly wind. These species include prickly sedge, limestone woundwort and Bithynian vetch. Others, such as the Radnor lily, also known as the early star of Bethlehem, are part of an exceptionally rich flora found on the Doleritic rocks of Radnorshire. This is a species more typical of dry limestone grasslands in central and southern Europe.

Then there are those species which grow nowhere else in the world – the endemics. Wales has its own eyebright in the mountains of Snowdonia, two whitebeams, one in Brecknock and the other near Crickhowell, and the South Stack fleawort on the coast of Anglesey, for example. Equally significant are the many species which have their world headquarters in Wales, such as the ivy-leaved bellflower. This is present in roughly a third of Wales' 120 recording squares, although its numbers are declining. In Europe, it is extinct in Holland and very local elsewhere from Germany to Portugal.

Wales is special for its rarities, but it is also special for the abundance of ordinary, everyday plants which remain in plant-rich habitats such as mountain grasslands, moors, sand dunes, heaths, woods and wetlands. To put a figure on this, one quarter of the land area of Wales consists of indigenous plant communities. This compares with about 10% in England as a whole, and as little as 3% in some English counties. The extent of natural habitats also explains the richness of Wales' fungal flora, notably a large number of brightly coloured wax caps. Marine habitats off the coast are also full of plant life; hundreds of different seaweeds, sometimes growing in great quantity, support a wealth of marine life.

RECENT DECLINES

How much longer Wales will remain a land of flowers is open to question. If it can do so, the cultural and economic benefits in the long term will be great. Globally, two out of every three wild plants are likely to become extinct in the 21st century. It is now recognised that this environmental destruction is holding back, rather than advancing, human development.

ABOVE *The medicinal virtues of bladderwrack are mainly due to its iodine content.*

Natural habitats classified as rough grazings made up 60% of the area of Wales before the last war. Mountain pastures, heaths, bogs and upland grassland were included in this definition. New machinery, drainage, ploughing and direct drilling techniques have converted most rough grazings into improved pasture, managed intensively. Native vegetation classified as rough grazings now occupies about 20% of the land area of Wales. Other habitats, such as sand dunes, lowland grasslands and native woodlands, add another 5%.

These habitats have also declined over the past 50 years, although at different rates. The loss of flower-rich grasslands has been almost total, while some sand dunes have been developed for tourism or agriculture. The tide may now have turned for deciduous woodlands, although many were underplanted with conifers after the last war, and grazing animals still prevent natural regeneration in some woods.

Botanical records show how fast Wales' flora is declining in the face of intensive agriculture and other human impacts. In the county of Radnorshire 46 species have become extinct since 1880, and similar levels of loss have occurred elsewhere.

A harmonious partnership with nature has not been a feature of the 20th century. Human appetites for short-term, unsustainable development have been fulfilled at the expense of the natural world. In the process, the workaday relationships between plants and people have been disrupted, and cultural connections have been erased.

RESTORING EDEN

The garden is a meeting point between nature and culture – a place where nature and human endeavour can coexist in harmony. Bruised and battered by the last century and apprehensive about what the present one will bring, we are drawn to the garden as a source of sanctuary, restoration and healing.

The National Botanic Garden of Wales has set itself a bold purpose: to be a new kind of institution, trailing a new way of operating, built on sustainable principles, and showing that people can live in a sustainable way and change their lifestyles. If it achieves this, it will show the way towards a new dimension of co-operation and coexistence; one which extends beyond our fellow human beings to the plants and animals with which we have evolved.

This exploration of relationships is at the heart of a new synthesis of ideas, embracing the humanities, philosophy, the liberal arts and social sciences; which recognises that we are part of a web of life which has evolved over many millennia; we sever the threads that bind us at our own cost.

I will end where I began, with the hope that the National Botanic Garden will be a place where we can bridge the gap between culture and nature, that it will celebrate the richness and abundance of the Welsh flora, and challenge its continuing erosion. Through the linking of new ideas and influences, and with a conservation ethic at its heart, the Garden should be a stimulus to practical action for a biodiverse future. Perhaps it will also help us to see ourselves as part of that diversity.

RIGHT *The changing colours of Snowdonia National Park have much to do with the area's high rainfall. Snowdon is the wettest plane in Britain, and this brings great benefit for plant growth.*

D E S

I G N

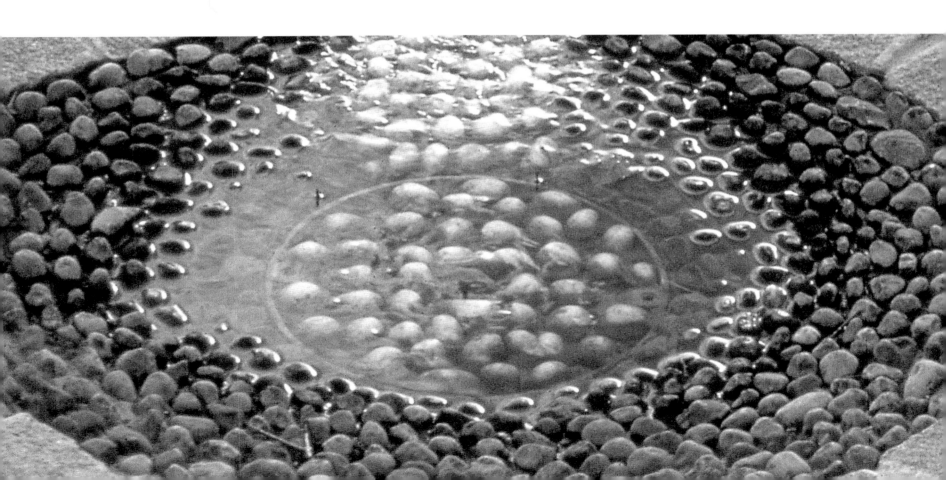

THE CREATION OF THE GREAT GLASSHOUSE

Foster and Partners

The midwife of Modernist architecture was botany. Not only because the pioneers of modern design advocated a visual language based upon an organic response to function, but because the origins of a truly functional architecture are to be found in the design of the botanical glasshouses that emerged in the first half of the 19th century. In these buildings formal expression grew naturally from practical requirements; their underlying structure and methods of construction were made transparent and celebrated; and materials were employed for their inherent qualities and never disguised.

PIONEERING STRUCTURE

No plant took greater pride of place within the glasshouse than the palm – the 'prince of plants'. Occurring in more than 1,000 species palms can reach heights of up to 30 metres/100 feet and their fan-like leaves can grow to 9 metres/30 feet and more. This was to dictate the form and scale of the first glasshouses. The design of these earliest artificial environments grew directly from the needs – light, heat, humidity – of the plants they were to house, and were conceived not by architects or engineers but by a new breed of horticulturists, Joseph Paxton being chief amongst them.

The challenge of creating glass buildings of great height and span, made up of mass-produced components – capable, if necessary, of being easily dismantled and re-erected – could be

met only with the accelerated development of new technologies spawned by the Industrial Revolution. Significantly, the design of glasshouses acted as a forceful lever on technological change. Paxton himself was to push the glass industry to new levels of output and standards of production in the realisation of his Crystal Palace for the Great Exhibition of 1851.

The marriage of wrought iron and glass, which the Crystal Palace celebrated, was in time adapted for covered markets and shopping arcades. But it also led inexorably to the soaring structures that are amongst the triumphs of late 19th-century engineering: the exhibition halls and train sheds that provided 20th-century designers with models for a truly functional modern architecture.

It was the legacy of another Paxton – Sir William – that provided the germ for the National Botanic Garden of Wales, and its three new buildings – the Glasshouse, Energy Centre and Gatehouse. The establishment of this conservation project called for buildings that would be exemplary in their sensitivity to environmental concerns.

The new Glasshouse is the centrepiece of the project, containing more than a thousand plant species – many endangered – from mediterranean climates throughout the world including South Africa, South Western Australia, the Canary Islands, Chile and California. The building takes the form of a dome, with an

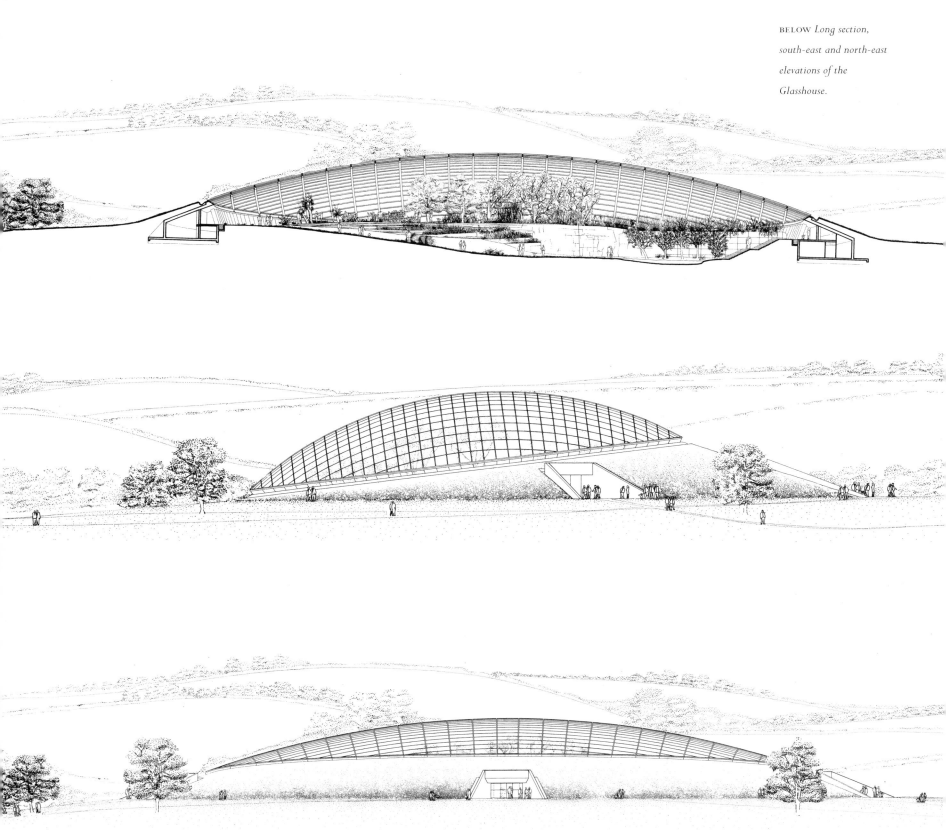

elliptical plan measuring 95 by 55 metres, that seems to grow from the surrounding valley like a glass hillock, echoing the undulations of the Welsh landscape. Its spare, elegant structure is designed to minimise materials and maintenance and maximise transparency, allowing the greatest transmission of light to the plants.

A range of factors – topographical, technical and aesthetic – informed the precise location, scale, form and structure of the Glasshouse. Even the materials to be used (for a glasshouse at the end of the 20th century need not be clad with glass) were chosen in the course of a lengthy consultation, in which various options were subjected to intense debate and to rigorous testing.

Design is a dialectical process. The proposed structure of a building might suggest the use of a particular material. The maximum dimensions in which that material is available might lead to changes in the structure, and so on. Nowhere has this been

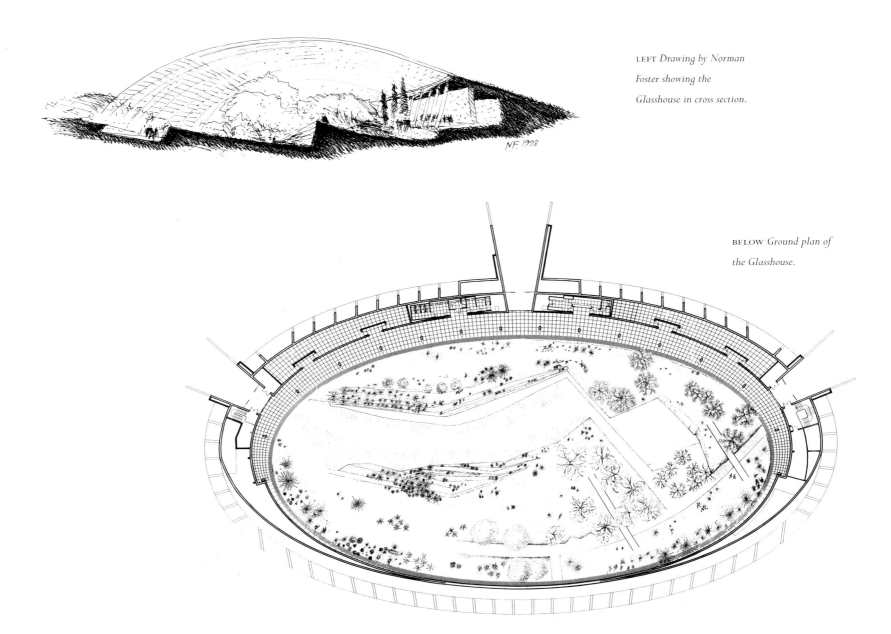

LEFT *Drawing by Norman Foster showing the Glasshouse in cross section.*

BELOW *Ground plan of the Glasshouse.*

truer than in the design of the Glasshouse. The end result may appear simple, but this simplicity is the result of a process of continuous refinement.

We initially investigated a number of different possible shapes for the building, including a dome based on a circular plan and a traditional, vaulted structure. The elliptical plan that was ultimately chosen makes a more subtle intervention in the landscape. There was also a historical precedent at Middleton for this shape. The footprint of an oval formal garden was clearly discernible in the grounds south of where Middleton Hall once stood and it was decided to locate the Glasshouse on this historical site.

The oval base of the dome is tilted to the south, allowing views over the adjacent meadows, and creating a sense of continuity with the landscape from inside the building. On the northern side are three entrances, which appear to be cut into the hillside. These portals form part of the concrete supporting structure that is completely hidden from view by a covering of turf.

Within this structure are a public concourse, a cafeteria,

ABOVE *Interior view of the 1:75 scale presentation model with early landscape studies.*

RIGHT *The 1:750 scale model was an important tool in securing the necessary funds to build the Great Glasshouse.*

educational spaces, lavatories and the subterranean service installations. Its solid construction protects the interior from cold northerly winds and so helps minimise the building's heating requirements. The interior walls curve in two directions; they vary in height along their length and lean at seventy degrees to the horizontal.

The roof structure comprises 24 hollow, tubular steel arches, 32.5 centimetres in diameter, that spring from the concrete ring beam, reaching to a maximum height of 15 metres at the apex of the dome. Because the roof curves in two directions, only the central arches rise close to perpendicular. The other arches lean at progressively steep angles, so creating a dynamic sense of movement. The inclined arches are propped by tubular members of 11.5-centimetre diameter, resulting in a minimal structure that is strong yet flexible. The intersections of the arches and members support a purpose-developed aluminium glazing system designed to satisfy the roof's complex technical requirements.

HEAT AND WATER

Because each of the steel arches meets the concrete ring beam at a unique angle they are attached by means of identical stainless-steel ball-and-socket joints. These avoid the need for special connections – which would have been costly and complicated – and they bring another benefit: as the steel arches expand and contract in response to changes in temperature, the rotation of the balls within the sockets absorbs the resulting stresses.

The Glasshouse, Energy Centre and Gatehouse together crystallise themes and concerns that have been central to our approach since the earliest days of the practice, resulting in buildings that are sustainable and ecologically sound.

The shell of the Glasshouse consists of laminated trapezoidal panels. The outer layer is of toughened glass; 147 of its panels open

RIGHT *The aluminium glazing system sits above the arches, shedding water for recycling.*

ABOVE *The main structural arches are fixed to the Glasshouse's concrete base by means of stainless-steel ball-and-socket joints.*

97

LEFT *The glass roof allows maximum light to reach the plants, but overheating is avoided through computer-controlled glazing panels which open to ventilate the building.*

BELOW *The Energy Centre, which heats the Glasshouse, burns timber trimmings from the Botanic Garden.*

automatically in response to internal and external environmental sensors to allow natural ventilation and to avoid overheating in the summer. The framework of panels is designed to channel rainwater into two 70,000-litre tanks that supply 'grey water' for irrigating plants and flushing lavatories.

The Glasshouse is heated in part by a biomass boiler – a modern wood-chip combustion plant – located in the Energy Centre. It burns timber trimmings and prunings from the Garden and prepared waste supplied through agreements with landfill contractors. The flue gases emitted contain negligible amounts of sulphur and nitrogen oxides when compared to emissions from burning oil. Furthermore, the carbon dioxide emitted during the burning process is broadly equivalent to the amount absorbed by the growing plant during its lifetime, creating a carbon dioxide cycle close to equilibrium.

The Energy Centre is a simple enclosure faced with Canadian western red cedar, a cladding that is also used on the Gatehouse

that greets the public at the entrance to the Botanic Gardens. The form of the Gatehouse, with its shallow inverted conical roof that funnels rainwater into a central pool, builds on the pure geometry of the Glasshouse and Energy Centre. The latter has large windows on one side, which allow visitors to observe the preparation and combustion processes, creating an additional opportunity for the Garden's educational programme.

The Glasshouse is the latest in a family of buildings that have posed the challenge of enveloping a large space within a transparent skin. In the late 1970s we collaborated with Richard Buckminster Fuller on the design of a pavilion for the International Energy Expo 82 in Knoxville, Tennessee. Fuller (known affectionately as 'Bucky') was a polymath – philosopher, poet, inventor, environmentalist, and engineer – whose seemingly inexhaustible ideas were far ahead of their time. The transparent tensile structure that was proposed for Knoxville incorporated a host of energy-saving features – including solar heating and

cooling – that would have produced an entirely self-sustaining internal environment.

An important factor in determining the shape of the Glasshouse was the challenge of resolving the structural complications of the toroidal geometry that would result from the three-dimensional extrapolation of the elliptical plan to create a dome. The torus form is prevalent throughout the natural world and has a satisfyingly simple elegance – many fruits, for example apples and oranges, have toroidal geometries, as does the Earth's magnetic field. But calculating co-ordinates on a toroidal surface is very complex and it has only recently become practical for architects to build such forms with the aid of sophisticated computer-aided design (CAD) software.

The design and construction of the building called for an unprecedented level of co-operation between the architects, engineers and building contractors with regard to knowledge of materials and construction techniques. It also required an

ABOVE *The shape of the Glasshouse echoes the undulating hills of the surrounding landscape.*

unconventional approach to generating instructions for the manufacturers and craftsmen who would make the building's various components. Conventional architectural drawings were used, but were only effective as an explanatory back-up to a three-dimensional computer model generated by a database of mathematical calculations. We had already gained some expertise in resolving toroidal geometries – the design and construction of the toroidal concrete roof of the American Air Museum at Duxford, for example, required innovative solutions that were built upon at Middleton.

As at Duxford, all design information about the Glasshouse was fed into a CAD model which was constantly updated throughout the construction process, in response to new calculations, and distributed to all the contractors involved. The CAD model was crucial in calculating the dimensions of each component: the varying lengths of the arches, the nineteen different basic sizes of glass panels for the roof and the four moulds that were employed to cast the concrete base. It served not only as an electronic drawing board, but also as an indispensable construction tool.

In designing the Glasshouse we strove for the simplicity and honesty of its early 19th-century forebears: its construction techniques and forms are based upon a keen understanding of functional and structural requirements and like those early buildings it is reliant upon the latest technology. You will recall that glass has a cutting edge. Just as the pioneering 19th-century glasshouses would have been inconceivable without the advances of the Industrial Revolution, the Middleton Glasshouse could not have been realised economically without the revolution in information technology of the late 20th century. It has given us the means to create an entirely new architectural form.

THE GLASSHOUSE

The architect's vision, an inclined ellipse,

three hundred tons of steel and glass

and an ice-dome rises among the slopes

above the Tywi. From the wilderness

that grew in the foot-print of a lost forecourt

where Paxton's house once stood, this oval

cathedral of geometry and light

constructed from hoops of tubular steel

and a thousand sheets of rain-washed glass.

Gillian Clarke

ABOVE *The Gatehouse is covered by an inverted conical roof, which funnels rainwater into a sculpture by Marion Kalmus at the building's centre.*

OPPOSITE *Nature meets advanced technology in the Glasshouse.*

INTERIOR LANDSCAPE
OF THE GLASSHOUSE

Peter Culley (for Gustafson Porter)

In July 1997 the National Botanic Garden of Wales approached Gustafson Porter, the European office of Kathryn Gustafson and Neil Porter and asked us to create a landscape in which the Garden could support a collection of plant species from the mediterranean climatic zones of the world. These species would derive from parts of Chile, south western Australia, California, southern Europe and northern Africa, and South Africa.

The context for this interior landscape was to be an elliptical area of ground, 95 metres × 55 metres × 16 metres high, within Foster and Partners' 100 metre-long single span Great Glasshouse. The approximate size of the area was 3,500 square metres.

Kathryn Gustafson was invited to Foster and Partners' office to meet with Professor Charles Stirton and Ivor Stokes of the Garden, and Spencer de Grey of Fosters, to discuss possible responses to the brief. Kathryn was shown images of the types of environments and plants that the National Botanic Garden was interested in accommodating within the Great Glasshouse.

It became clear that the evocative aspirations of the project were going to be as important a consideration as the specific environmental growing conditions of the landscape. The Garden envisaged a landscape which would embrace an ambitious range of features: vertical walls in sun and shade, dry and wet; areas which were laid bare for much of the year but which had specific annual growth at other times; temperature differentials between high cliff faces and protected valleys, and plants which grow with little water for much of the year and others which would never be allowed to dry out. They spoke of running, flooding and stagnant water, as well as water courses which at times would be wet and at other times dry. Plants would include regions of olive groves, acacia forest and flowering annuals.

A later visit to a quarry, local to the Garden site, further reinforced Charles and Ivor's aspirations for a clearly defined 'hands-on' sense of space, which could allow for elements of discovery and surprise.

As a response to both the brief and Foster & Partners' design for the Glasshouse, the first move was to create a landscape which pushed down into the ground in the centre of the space by 5 metres at its lowest point, forming a stone-faced ravine. From here we created a gentle build-up of the remaining landscape from the original ground level, giving an overall maximum drop of 6 metres. As one enters the building from the west entrance, the eye is drawn down into the ravine, and the perception is of a landscape enfolded by the building. The roof then becomes the sky which holds the landscape within it.

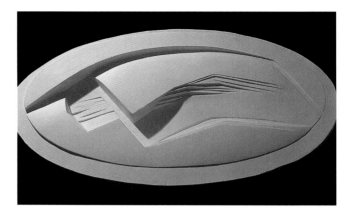

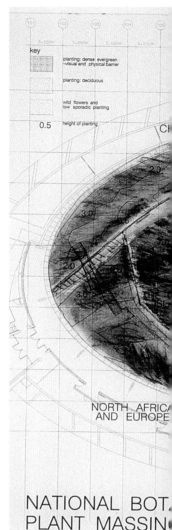

ABOVE *Kathryn Gustafson produced the first model of the scheme in her studio in Vashon Island, near Seattle, in August 1997. She works in clay, allowing the forming and reforming of ideas before finalising with measured accuracy. Here is a plaster cast of the clay model, a rubber mould having been used to first create a negative. The form is essential for further development of the design within the studio. One can begin to see the importance of the sun path through the three-dimensional quality of the form — this model depicts the scheme in morning sun. The process is one we often use and the sculptural quality of the work exists in the form of the model, as well as in that of the finished landscape.*

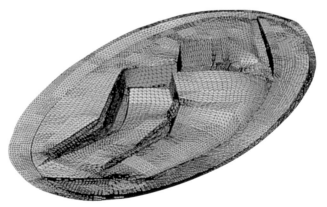

ABOVE *Senses of a natural landscape are fundamental to the project design. Here, a feeling of being 'inside' is based on a scale relationship which overpowers in the vertical dimension. Light and view 'out' may be ahead as well as from above. Experiences of opened and closed space can be felt both undercover or in open air. This sketch by Kathryn Gustafson is one of many developed in response to the need to absorb natural references into the structured, built resolution of enclosure, route, view and surface.*

ABOVE *Here, the plaster model has been digitally scanned with the type of laser equipment often used in current animation technology. This provided a flexible computer model which could be scaled up to life-size, remodelled and used to produce detailed information to further develop the design. Site co-ordinates were established directly from the redrawn model. This formed a powerful presentation tool in communicating the complexities of the form.*

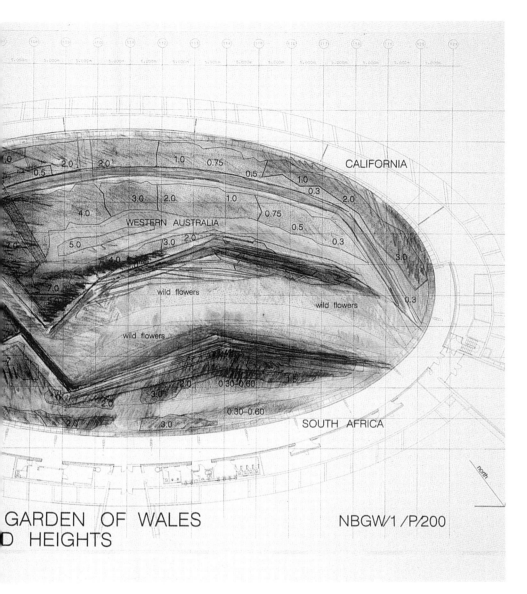

CALIFORNIA

2.0 2.0 1.0 0.75

0.5 0.5

1.0

0.3

3.0 2.0 1.0 2.0

4.0 0.75

WESTERN AUSTRALIA 0.5

5.0 3.0 2.0 0.3

4.0 3.0

wild flowers

wild flowers 0.3

wild flowers

2.0 0.30-0.60 1.0

3.0

2.0 0.30-0.60

2.0 3.0

SOUTH AFRICA

north

GARDEN OF WALES NBGW/1 /P/200
D HEIGHTS

ABOVE *A framework for planting was set up as a result of discussions
with the National Botanic Garden and the Design team. Conceptually,
the planting had to work with the form of the landscape to ensure a
coherence which was not disrupted by the need for individual exhibits.
This drawing was prepared by Kathryn Gustafson and Ivor Stokes,
Director of Horticulture at the Garden, as a way forward for a planting
scheme based on colour, height and density. Within the overall space,
regions are split into South Western Australia, South Africa, California,
Chile and the Mediterranean Basin. Together these five regions form
a whole.*

STONE, WATER AND PLANTS

Rock terraces of a warm white sandstone accompany the movement of the ground down to the 'sheer walls', which are faced with the same stone. The terraces form a stepped connection between high and low, and water flows along one side of the resultant 'valley floor' over bands of sandstone slabs. As the ravine reaches its lowest point, it turns a corner and pulls down into a narrow gorge only 2.5 metres wide, bordered by water, before opening out again into the flooded valley floor which has a pool and marginal planting areas. One wall has a constant sheet of water falling over its partly textured and partly sawn-faced surface into the pool below. This wall begins the day in sharp relief, becoming fully lit by early afternoon. The opposite wall has areas of its surface which are permanently wet and receive sun only in the early morning. Slabs of stone along the margin of the lake are angled to collect and disperse water across their surfaces. Here and in the other areas of the scheme, water is seen to emerge from defined but silent source points, washing over surfaces that cross its path.

A ramp with a 1 in 20 gradient creates a gently curved descending route on the south side of the space between entrance level and the pool and water wall areas. Stone steps lead back from the pool to the concourse of the building at the east entrance, while two pedestrian bridges link two higher areas of ground above.

The ground plane is finished in crushed gravel scree of varying coarseness obtained from a light coloured sandstone to match that of the rock faces. The surface is kept fine at the point of entry to the landscape and becomes coarser as one moves further in. A retaining wall along the south side of the ramp uses the same stone packed into gabions. The stones are laid by hand to create the face of this wall and reduce in size progressively towards the top, further accentuating the impression of height and depth.

Some of the stone wall surfaces are textured with a split-faced finish, some are sawn-faced while others are a mixture of the two, with intentional fissures and cracks to achieve a delicate balance between the quality of sun and shadow play, natural geological reference and visual clarity.

The multiple horizons and overlapping routes created by the stone and water arrangements begin to stretch the scale of the space, and this is reinforced in the planting and ground finishes.

LEFT *The watercourse guides the visitor along the narrowest point of the ravine and makes a sharp turn into the pool beyond. The gabion wall in the background, more often used in road construction, is reinterpreted using handlaid frontface stone of larger grade at the bottom than the top, increasing the perception of height. The sound of the water rushing over the stone and its cooling effect provide a welcome relief in the hotter days of the year.*

ABOVE *The idea of a multiple horizon was central to the scheme. A multiple horizon both visually extends the feeling of the space — blurring the finite quality of the context — and draws the visitor from one 'region' to the next. Here the framed element of water flowing over the farthest face brings an extra quality of light and sound play.*

The opened vents in the roof admit a contrasting quality of light, reminding us of the environmental filter which the Glasshouse provides. The shadow play of the roof members on the vertical surfaces of the landscape is an unpredictable performance, changing throughout the day and further challenging the perceptions of scale within the space. In seeking to create an exterior experience in an internal situation, roof becomes sky for the landscape within.

ABOVE AND RIGHT *Water is seen to appear from silent source points and move down the faces of the stone on the seepage wall. The white German sandstone used on all vertical surfaces takes on differing qualities with water and sun. The outcrops on the cliff faces take forms outside the simple placement of individual stones. Geological reference to natural form is made but there is no attempt to replicate nature.*

The planting follows a strategy unused in other botanic gardens; it is based on form, density and colour and not exclusively on plant type or regions of the world. The coherence of the landscape is created on both experiential and botanical levels. A planting framework was devised by Kathryn Gustafson and Ivor Stokes at Kathryn's studio in Seattle, early on in the design stage. Low yellow-greens (3–4 metres) rise up to more densely planted silver-greens (7–10 metres) and fall again slightly to dark greens (7 metres) as one moves into and above the ravine. The lowest points in the landscape respond to the highest points in the Great Glasshouse, and support the highest density of planting. Visitors move from country to country, but always within the sensation of an integrated environment.

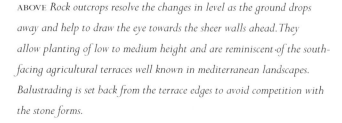

ABOVE *Rock outcrops resolve the changes in level as the ground drops away and help to draw the eye towards the sheer walls ahead. They allow planting of low to medium height and are reminiscent of the south-facing agricultural terraces well known in mediterranean landscapes. Balustrading is set back from the terrace edges to avoid competition with the stone forms.*

ABOVE *Prior to planting within the Great Glasshouse, members of the National Botanic Garden, including Director of Horticulture Ivor Stokes and Curator Wolfgang Bopp, inspect some of the specimens collected from the different regions of the world.*

ABOVE RIGHT *Glandular hairs help these leaves conserve water in the mediterranean heat.*

Thus the bridges and their supporting structures, the steps, balustrading and lighting hardware are all perceived as non-natural elements, brought in as a 'later' layer to allow access to the landscape. Galvanised metal, rough-sawn timber, cleanly cut stone and fairfaced concrete are employed in a simple but considered technology.

The key to the project's success is to attempt to create a coherent landscape within the confines of a building; the display of plants is more than simply the sum of its botanical exhibits. The relationship between building and landscape is reassessed while issues of hierarchy between the human and the natural worlds are raised and tested.

People are free to move over much of the ground surface to either side of the main routes. Protective fences are limited only to the edges of the ravines and are set back a minimum of 1 metre to reduce the visual impact. Elsewhere, delineation of paths is limited to the use of larger and less compacted stone and selected planting.

A COHERENT LANDSCAPE

In creating the interior landscape, our aim was to make sure that links to the natural landscape were always through reference and not replica, with a clear awareness that the landscape is a combination of both artificial and natural elements.

The concept for the various elements of metal and woodwork was based on the idea of inhabiting a given form.

ABOVE *The bridges, balustrading, boardwalk and main routes were perceived as access elements — a secondary network which would allow the visitor to negotiate the landscape. We approached each in a fundamental way, and the use of materials was limited to galvanised metal and mesh, rough-sawn timber and fairfaced concrete. Fine stone is compacted to form public routes within the larger-grade scree mulch covering the planted areas.*

THE ART OF LANDSCAPE DESIGN

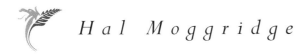

Hal Moggridge

Gardens are understood through their contents and their geometric organisation. The contents of the National Botanic Garden of Wales will be built up by the permanent staff in response to aspirations which will develop over time. The task of the landscape designer was to conceive of a place comprehensible and appealing to visitors that was also available for the future creation of varied garden and scientific uses. The first phase of construction consisted of developing the core of this place ready for the Botanic Garden slowly to come to life; at the same time there had to be beauties enough to delight early visitors.

We knew of the project's purpose and location by the end of 1994. Our task was to imagine and describe a new garden to gain support from the Millennium Commission and other potential donors.

THE DESIGNER'S TASK

The art of landscape design is always that of renovating an existing place for new life. At Middleton the remnant of a fine, older designed landscape was still present, though hardly perceptible. Scrub woodland had invaded the sites of former lakes, placing mass where openness and reflected light had been intended. The original house, the focus of the original design, had vanished. Such structures as remained were either former outbuildings or the crumbly remnants of walled enclosures, so gappy that they had become continuous with their surroundings.

The imagination had to recapture in the mind the physical reality of how these remnants would appear when repaired, and then add to them new elements needed for the future garden. Botanical ideas already defined in words by those who had initiated the scheme had to be projected into physical organisation and location. The design has mingled remnants from the past with places for the future so that together they become a seamless whole.

ORDERLY LAYOUT FOR FUTURE USERS

There are two principal users of the Botanic Garden: visitors and permanent staff. The permanent staff need to have an area of the Garden in which visitors are greeted as well as an area which is private, only available to visitors by invitation. Many of the permanent staff spend much of their time working indoors. Visitors come to the Garden in large numbers on popular days, and so are bound to approach by the route most convenient for transport from outside. This is from the south, where there is easy access from the A48, which is a dual carriageway extension of the M4. The M4 itself passes close by mainline railway stations and populous South Wales, and leads on to the holiday region of south-west Wales.

The general organisation of the new Garden is therefore conceived as a processional movement for visitors from a point of arrival at the low-lying southern end of the Garden to its scientific

OPPOSITE A hidden geometry of open spaces criss-crosses the Garden, often giving unexpected views of the two eyecatchers shown in this picture — the Glasshouse nearby, or Paxton's Tower and the rolling hills beyond.

and cultural heart, where original buildings survive on higher ground. These are useful for permanent staff to work in and to receive and entertain visitors. This entertainment consists of both obvious provision, such as restaurant and shop, and of explanation of the cultural purposes of the Botanic Garden by exhibition, display and tours. Between the point of entry for visitors and the heart of the Garden a new processional route, The Broadwalk, has been built, which functions as a backbone for the Garden.

FOCAL POINTS

Every landscape needs climax points to exalt the spirit. Special garden spaces have been created by adapting and restoring remnants of the earlier design, the fascinating Walled Garden and the series of riverine lakes winding along the valley in the centre of the site. A large garden such as this also needs variety of intensity, places to receive large numbers of people with numerous points of interest, and remoter places where more delicate aspects of nature can be encountered in solitude. The final design gives a central, more intensive core on either side of The Broadwalk, with larger areas beyond, including the Woodlands of the World to the south, parkland and woodland to the north and farmland to the east.

The given site at Middleton provided no main focal point. The very first design plan, which was completed by March 1995, therefore proposed that a new glasshouse should be built on top of the hill, a little to the south of the original site of the house. This was to be the eyecatcher and the focal point of a visit to the new garden. Thus the Great Glasshouse is offset to the east side of The Broadwalk as the largest element in the group of buildings surrounding the point of arrival at the top of the walk. This offsetting means that the sheltered, but elevated space surrounded by buildings, rather than any individual building, is the heart of the Garden. It also ensures that the Glasshouse is prominent when viewed obliquely from afar.

The visitor approaches the heart of the Garden gradually. The landscape is designed to be a sequence of poetic perceptions of the place and of the ideas underlying the Botanic Garden. Order and clarity is provided by the simplicity of the line of The Broadwalk – a strong visual axis leading directly from the Gatehouse to the heart of the site.

ARRIVAL

Whether cycling, travelling by private car, or coming by bus or rail, visitors are guided by road signs or maps to a small roundabout to the south of the Garden. There, they turn onto the private driveway, the journey along which introduces the site. Ahead, but slightly to the right, is a full-face view of the Glasshouse, its shining form echoing the curvature of the surrounding hills. Thus even while still in their cars, visitors will know their destination. Beyond are the rolling hills of the Tywi Valley, with a picturesque view of Paxton's Tower also revealed from the entrance driveway. The road then sweeps round to the left, giving a frontal view towards the Gatehouse, before continuing into the car parks.

The car parks lie on low ground, slightly curvaceous in line. They are surrounded by spinnies of moisture-loving trees (alder and willow) which separate vehicles from the Garden and the countryside beyond. Visitors make their way in a slightly circuitous manner, so that a sense of interest in arrival is sustained, to the Gatehouse, where tickets and guidebooks are obtained and the Garden is entered.

At this point the full length of The Broadwalk is visible in front of the visitor, rising up towards the sky. At first it is a simple straight path, then the eye is attracted upwards as the path curves and rises, still visible as a whole, undulating on either side of its uninterrupted central line. The spread of the whole core area of the Garden is visible from this point.

THE CORE OF THE GARDEN

The centre of the Garden is subdivided into areas distinct in purpose and character, each occupying a unique part of the rich topography of the site, either a rounded hill or sheltered hollow. These areas will be seen from the point of entry to the Garden at the Gatehouse (see pages 116–17 for plan).

On the far left is a rocky hill designated for moorland rock gardens. The hill is crowned by a small copse which has been shaped carefully to stand in eye-catching silhouette against the sky. The foot of its steep eastern flank is thickly wooded, creating a deep shade above which the Moorland Hill rises. This wood both separates the Moorlands of the World from the gardens below, thus emphasising their sense of height, and shelters the lower lower gardens from west winds. Beside the hilltop copse, a modern windmill is planned. The windmill symbolises air and provides energy to lift water to the hilltop so that a moorland stream can flow down the hill's flank. From the entrance this will be visible as a distant waterfall dropping over an existing cliff, where there was once a hilltop quarry. The waterfall will drop onto a ledge to fall as a scatter of spray into a deep pool in the hollow of the former quarry; from there the stream will tumble and twinkle down the hill, providing typical moorland stream habitats, before dropping down an artificial cascade into the top of the Walled Garden, which is beside The Broadwalk.

As well as a windmill, there will be a solar panel on the hilltop to provide energy from the air to lift water on stiller summer days. Only on certain cold, still winter days will there be a lack of energy to lift the water. On such days the moorland stream will barely flow, perhaps dripping over its cascades into icicles. From the Gatehouse, distant people will appear small, traversing the Moorland Hill along a network of paths which meander amongst rock exposures. These exposures will be made by cutting into the living rock that lies near the surface.

Low ground between the Moorland Hill, the Walled Garden and the entrance has been developed into a meadow surrounded by native Welsh habitats, spinnies and wetlands. This is separated from the Gatehouse by an irregular pool surrounded by native rushes and reeds, which acts both as a barrier and a silt trap where the stream brings water into the site.

The principal eye-catching view from the entrance is to the right of the long line of The Broadwalk and towards the curve of the Glasshouse, which crowns a rounded hill swelling upwards from the flank of The Broadwalk.

BELOW *A diagonal view down The Broadwalk, near the top where the rill snakes in tight curves.*

THE DOUBLE WALLED GARDEN

Below the Moorlands of the World are the walled enclosures of the historic Walled Garden. This occupies a southwesterly slope leading up to Millennium Square, the space surrounded by buildings at the heart of the Garden. The intricate series of historic walled enclosures is being restored as a setting for changing gardens and expresses the current ideas being promoted by the Botanic Garden. The 2-hectare Walled Garden consists of a rectangular stone outer wall 2.3 metres high, surrounding a taller, squarish, brick-walled inner garden at its southern end.

The inner garden has rounded corners and remnants of a peach house on one wall; outside it there are three narrow slip gardens between brick and stone walls, and another squarish garden on rising ground between the brick wall and Millennium Square. The western slip garden is particularly interesting as it contains unusual sloping beds facing south-east. The moorland stream enters the north-west side of the Walled Garden to feed a series of ornamental pools which fall gently to a bottom catchment pool from which water is pumped uphill again. .

RIGHT Visitors on the walks which meander through the long perennial herbaceous border can enjoy the strong floral colour of the planting between The Broadwalk and the Walled Garden.

The hill dropping from the Glasshouse is a simple combination of grasslands and trees. The grasslands are partly mown (particularly towards the west, for access and enjoyment in summer by visitors), and partly grown as flowery meadowlands. Paths sweep round the hill in gentle curving lines and visitors can be seen moving round the hill along these paths at different levels. During the design period between our original layout plan and final design, there were proposals for ambitious cascades falling from the Glasshouse down the hill. However, we realised that these could be a distraction from the composition of the whole, in an area where the repose of simplicity is desirable to set off richer features of the landscape. Water features are now a unifying element along The Broadwalk instead. The hillside beside The Broadwalk is composed of simple greens of mown grass in wide glades, rising to the Glasshouse, and with a few trees standing in flowery rougher ground. During the early development of the first phase of the design, while the area around the Glasshouse and the hill below it were developed in a serene and simple way, the detail of the surroundings of The Broadwalk and lake edge were made more crusty and rough in colour and texture.

A lake, Pwll yr Ardd, lies between the foot of the Glasshouse hillside and the Gatehouse. This has been adapted from an historic triangle to a sweet curve, reshaped to reflect the silver arc of the Glasshouse in the silver water lying along the valley. On its east bank is the Hyder Water Discovery Centre – a facility for children to learn about water environments. This lake stands at the head of a series of long riverine lakes along a zig-zag shaped valley. Pwll yr Ardd lies parallel with The Broadwalk on a north/south axis and slips under a small bridge into the next lake, Llyn Uchaf on an east/west axis. The water then drops over a cascade to flow into Llyn Canol, a branched lake which turns north to tumble over a second cascade. Ultimately, there will be a larger north-south lake, Llyn Mawr, lying against a dam. This is elongated to form a long canal leading to a stepped cascade and dropping into the valley of the Afon Gwynon to the north. These lakes, always catching the sky in reflections and attracting the eye towards the valley from higher ground above, are a revival of the historic system of lakes at Middleton Hall. Only the headwater, Pwll yr Ardd, has been reshaped to suit the new landscape being created around The

Broadwalk for the Botanic Garden. The banks of Llyn Uchaf are rough in texture. Towards the west, rich native meadow grows long, so that blue scabious, cream meadowsweet and other wild flowers can flourish. Where the Glasshouse hill drops sharply down to the main body of the lake, the sweeping paths subdivide into a series of triangles planted ornamentally, with access to the waterside at circular viewpoints and a waterside path. Groups of trees have been retained along the shoreline, selected to divide the waterside into shaded masses and open spaces for views and sky reflection.

A rounded hill rises from the southern side of the upper lakes, Llyn Canol and Llyn Uchaf. Here in the Woodlands of the World trees and shrubs grow between open rides commanding long northerly views. Sample habitat analogues from temperate regions of each of the continents of the world are planned. This part of the Garden is extensive in character and will take time to develop; it is not part of the core of the Garden for visitors, but a place of calm atmosphere and seclusion for enjoyment on a third or fourth visit. It is also available for scientific field trials. This whole hill is screened from the lower part of The Broadwalk by a band of retained woodland on the east bank of Pwll yr Ardd, which frames the upward view towards the Glasshouse from the Gatehouse. Space is available for other extensive habitats to be developed on the northerly slopes beyond the Great Glasshouse; open meadowland, the shores of Llyn Mawr and a wooded valley already exist as a framework for these possibilities. To the east, farmland offers other future options.

THE GARDENS UNFOLDING ALONG THE BROADWALK

As visitors leave the Gatehouse they can see the wide spread of habitats described above, but are more aware of their direction of movement. They will know clearly where to go because they will be able to see their route ahead, with the fascinating arc of the Great Glasshouse visible beyond single trees on the right. The Broadwalk is unwavering in the directness of its clear central line. This central line leads upwards towards the sky, with destinations on both sides, so that a sense of variety and choice is sustained.

The Broadwalk is about 400 metres long and surfaced with pinkish gravel. Its lowest, southernmost length nearest the Gatehouse is gentle in tempo, to calm the spirit and settle visitors into a mood for visiting a garden as they leave the rush of the outer world behind. As The Broadwalk begins to rise up the slope towards Millennium Square and the surroundings of the Great Glasshouse, it becomes more intense in mood and complex in form, awakening a sense of expectation and interest.

In our first design, the lowest length of the walk curved on the level around the edge of Pwll yr Ardd, to a place from which the walk rose in a rigid line to the west of the hill. This design was then developed to unite the whole Broadwalk into a single straight central line for clarity. Now the first stretch of the walk is a straight causeway which moves simply across water and wetland to a white pebble circle, from which the Walk rises uphill in four curves, enriched by variety of detail.

Within the width of the Walk, there is a shallow rill, which begins at a cascade from a raised circular pool. It snakes down the hill in tight curves at the top, through two pools on the east side of the Walk, curves in a more gentle manner as the water descends the hill, and ends in a clockwise spiral, dropping into a fountain pool at the bottom of the hill. This water catches the light as it moves, but its movement does not hinder visitors. Between the west side of the Walk and the outer stone wall of the Walled Garden there is a long perennial herbaceous plantation, designed to display blocks of strong floral colour in a variety of combinations. The planting is interwoven with little irregular walks of soft, red sandstone gravel, so that visitors can meander close to the plants. Seats are set against the wall. An idea lost from early proposals, which may need to be reintroduced, provided for numerous shelters against the wall along the length of the Walk.

On the east side of the Walk there is a series of compositions of massive boulders on a stony base. Each group is from a different age of rock and is obtained from seven different geographical sources in Wales. The oldest rocks, from North Wales, are at the bottom of the Walk. The rock strata become younger as the hill is ascended, so that an extract from the geology of Wales is displayed in correct vertical sequence. The boulders also display the variety of shape and colour in natural minerals. They serve as seats upon

	Existing contours
	Existing woodland
	Woodland
	Specimen trees
	Shrub and herbaceous planting
	Bulb planting
	Mown grass
	Meadow and moorland
	Pathways
	Steps
	Rock outcrops

RIGHT *The Phase 1 layout plan, with contours at 2.5-metre centres. Visitors approach the car park from the south (left), then walk along The Broadwalk (centre), past restored lakes and uphill to the heart of the Garden (centre right). This is the scientific core which can also be approached privately from the north (top right). The white areas (top centre) are the Walled Garden and the Moorland Hill. This plan is drawn by Anthony Jellard, who was the key designer in the creation of the Phase 1 landscape on the ground.*

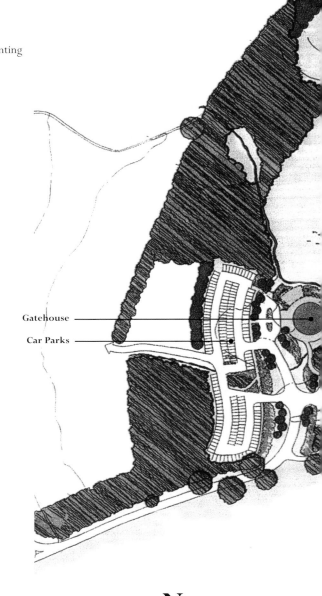

Gatehouse

Car Parks

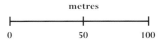

metres

0   50   100

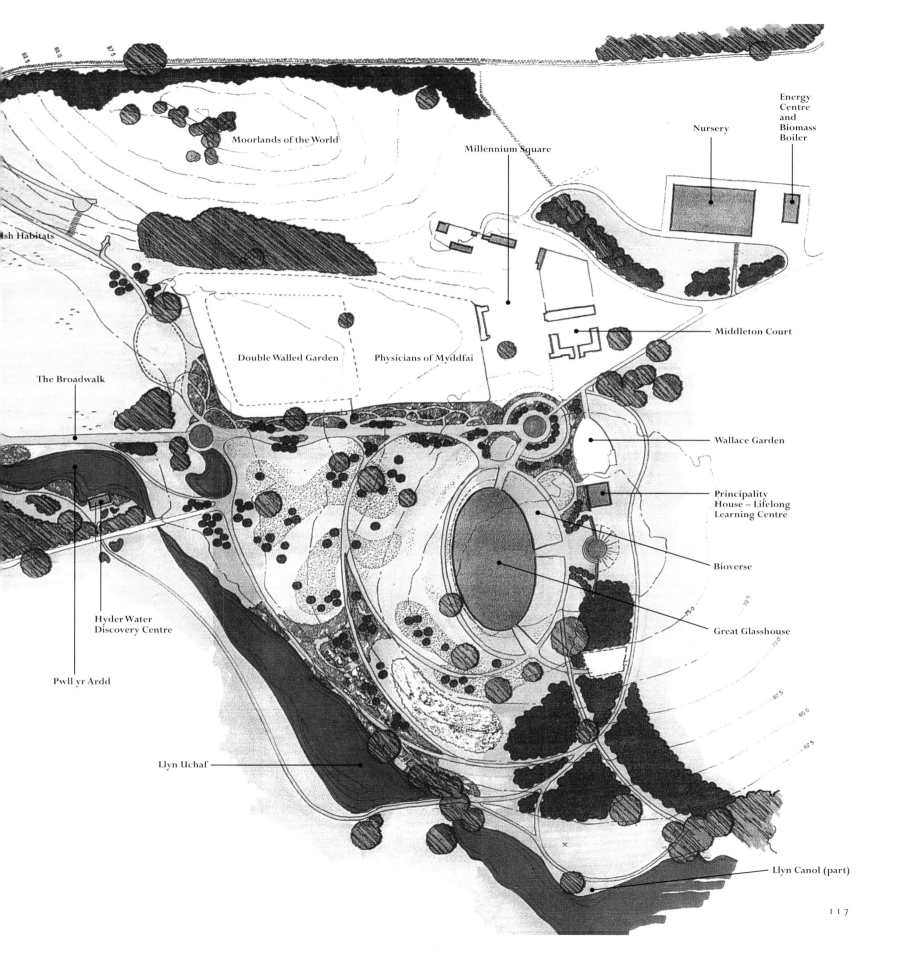

Moorlands of the World

Nursery

Energy Centre and Biomass Boiler

Millennium Square

ish Habitats

Middleton Court

The Broadwalk

Double Walled Garden

Physicians of Myddfai

Wallace Garden

Principality House – Lifelong Learning Centre

Bioverse

Great Glasshouse

Hyder Water Discovery Centre

Pwll yr Ardd

Llyn Uchaf

Llyn Canol (part)

OPPOSITE *The Broadwalk divides round a white pebble circle surrounding a fountain pool, into which the rill disappears in a clockwise spiral.*

which to rest or places for the young to climb and play. The groups of boulders have been arranged with great care, their bases well buried, so that each is a picturesque composition; this work displays the skill of the craftsmen who handled the machines that lifted the rocks, and of those who created the compositions.

The Broadwalk can be walked in about ten minutes, but visitors who want to really enjoy the setting will take half an hour. Views of the Glasshouse at various angles open and shut upon the eye as the Walk is followed upwards. From the Gatehouse the whole length of the Glasshouse can be seen between trees, with reflections in Pwll yr Ardd. From the bottom circle visitors have an almost unobstructed angled view across smooth mown grass. As the hill is ascended, the shining sweep of glass is seen from increasingly narrowing angles, until a true sideways view is reached near the top. Here, the heart of the Garden, Middleton Court (with the restaurant), can be reached to the left, with the exhibitions in the Glasshouse to the right.

The return journey down the hill offers a different series of views of water, trees and hills. However, it is more likely that visitors will return to the entrance by one of the variety of routes which loop off The Broadwalk along its meandering length. In the

future there will be ways through the Walled Garden, a downhill route along a shady path outside its high west wall, and hilltop routes over the rocky moorlands. On the east side of The Broadwalk visitors can enjoy a series of looping walks around the hillside below the Glasshouse and along the banks of Llyn Uchaf. A path crosses the dam of Llyn Uchaf, returning along the south side of the lake.

THE LIVING HEART OF THE GARDEN

Visitors reach the heart of the Garden as the climax of a journey which has prepared them to enjoy special places and activities. The buildings around and beyond Millennium Square, including the interior of the Glasshouse, comprise the technical, scientific and administrative centre of the Garden. This area is approached by members of staff privately from the north-west. They and their privileged guests have the satisfaction and day-to-day convenience of direct access to the working centre, with well-hidden car parking places near buildings. This separate access is also the service route for the Garden. Thus the practical needs of maintenance are not entangled with visitor movement. The service road gives access to 'back of house' facilities, where visitors will come only to see how the gardens are managed. The wood-fired boiler house, the essential range of greenhouses, sewage plant, outdoor nurseries and so on are situated in the large, and easily enlarged, compound to the north-west of Millennium Square.

ORDOVICIAN

Dolerite. Blue-stone. Rhyolite.

Fossil-less volcanic stone from the earth's dead core.

And Carmarthen silt strewn with the life-print

of shallow-water shells.

A stone splits clean as a conker,

and a trilobite looks at you

with four-hundred-and-sixty-five-year-old eyes.

Gillian Clarke

A GEOMETRIC WHOLE

Words can only describe a place sequentially, taking each part separately. Though landscapes are experienced in sequence, like sentences making up paragraphs, they are also understood by humans as totalities of space. The work of landscape art is comprehended and enjoyed as a balance of places together in space. Unity is given to the National Botanic Garden of Wales by certain geometries which underlie its elementary parts.

There is a geometry which derives from the relationship between design and topography. Each rounded hill is distinct in character and purpose: the Great Glasshouse surrounded by curving paths through grassland with open glades and free standing trees; the rocky moorland; the blocks of exotic vegetation of the Woodlands of the World in South Park Arboretum; and to the east the larger parkland agricultural hill. Each hollow shelters a specific feature too: the open Welsh meadow; the sloping Walled Garden; the sun-catching, wind-sheltered plateau at the heart of the gardens; the sequence of lakes along the valley and the secret wooded valley of Afon Gwynon to the north.

There is a geometry of spaces defined by blocks of woodland and buildings. The car parks are kept separate from the Garden by valley spinnies, punctuated at the point of entry by a building. The rocky Moorland Hill is separated from the Walled Garden below by a linear wood, giving shelter from wind. It is planned that the western edge of the Garden and its working areas will be contained by belts of trees. The heart of the Garden, in contrast, consists of spaces defined by surrounding buildings.

There is a geometry of pathways too. The straight spine of The Broadwalk explains and unites the whole. Main paths in each area lead to and from The Broadwalk in shapes related to their locality – forming a curve around the Glasshouse hill, linear beside and through the Walled Garden, zig-zagging and irregular on the rocky Moorland Hill. All parts of the Garden are accessible by paths with reasonable gradients for wheelchairs, buggies and maintenance vehicles. There is an inconspicuous but practical geometry of maintenance routes.

There is also a hidden geometry of open space across which different parts of the Garden can be viewed from one another. The various views of the Glasshouse from The Broadwalk and elsewhere are made available in this way. Paxton's Tower suddenly catches the eye from the south-west corner of the Garden, for instance. The Tower can also be glimpsed across Llyn Uchaf, or from the point where the line of The Broadwalk crosses the axis through the historic outbuildings. There are numerous places from which water surfaces can be enjoyed, shining where space lets sky into reflections. This pattern of linear open space, barely perceptible because only consisting of passages of air above various ground surfaces, gives comprehensibility and joy to the whole Garden.

LEFT *The rill appears from under a path. Lined with black and white cobbles and edged with setts, it is small enough to step over or for children to paddle safely.*

S C I E
AND S O

N C E

C I E T Y

SCIENCE IN THE BOTANIC GARDEN

Charles Stirton & Rhodri Griffiths

Think of a great garden. It is likely to be filled with beautiful plants, and it will probably have fine architectural features. It may be steeped in history too, and have been subject to waxing and waning fortunes during the course of its existence. It may have an educational programme. Its plants are likely to have been scientifically named and records may exist of their original geographical sources. Scientific research could even be among the garden's functions. However, it is unlikely that the garden which you have in mind includes all of these components. The National Botanic Garden of Wales will do all these things and more. Committed to linking nature with society, science with arts, and research with understanding and utility, the Garden has redefined the role of a garden to focus on issues which lie beyond the traditional garden fence. Our concern about plants now includes recent developments in agriculture and contemporary views of the environment. Hence, beyond what might be expected in a garden, you will also find conserved habitats at the National Botanic Garden of Wales, and socially and politically inspired features such as the Wallace Garden, which is devoted to the ethical problems of genetic modification.

Our Garden must recognise that the world is changing rapidly. Scientific advance proceeds at such a rate that most people find it difficult to understand what these changes may mean to their lives. Many fear these unknowns. Is there an opportunity, then, for a

OPPOSITE *The Hyder Water Discovery Centre with the Great Glasshouse in the background.*

RIGHT *Melaleuca* nesophila, *one of the thousands of mediterranean species in the Great Glasshouse.*

new scientific institution to help redress the imbalance? What can a new botanic garden being built at the turn of the new millennium do to help? Is there a unique opportunity for Wales to create a landmark national institution that looks afresh at the contract between citizens and institutions – one that is prepared to be innovative, exploring and caring? How can new botanical emphases and concerns extend the traditional function of a botanic garden?

Benefit to the peoples and the environments of Wales and the world is the underlying motivation for the world-class scientific research which the Garden is pursuing into the classification and conservation biology of plants and fungi. One of our key objectives is to inform our visitors about the relationship between plants and global wellbeing. These motives make of the Garden a place where all can learn about, understand, value, use, enjoy and care for plants and fungi as vital elements in maintaining a sustainable relationship with life on earth. There is a need to connect people to their environment and so enable them to participate in making decisions about their personal and communal preferred futures.

For these reasons, the Garden has taken its ethos from the aspirations of the Rio de Janeiro Earth Summit and Agenda 21, which was formulated at Rio. When coupled to the exciting prospects of an emergent confident Wales taking its place in the

OPPOSITE Hygrocybe coccinea, *the Scarlet Hood fungus.*

BELOW Rhododendron saluenense, *from Yunnan, China.*

ABOVE Magnolia grandiflora, *from the south east of the USA.*

THE SCIENCE PROGRAMME

The science programme has been designed to address questions of social and biological relevance. We are not interested in building an ivory tower. The Garden, as a charitable institution, does not receive any grant-in-aid from government. Thus, the research programme can only be sustained if it is capable of attracting financial support for each and every project. In competing for funds, we are constantly aware that the production of relevant and useful knowledge through well-planned research is the only way of sustaining our scientific work. We must avoid duplication with other organisations and academic institutions, and ensure that we develop our programme not only within a close-knit network of botanical research in Wales, but also within an international context. Our priorities, together with those of our funding bodies, do not allow us to languish in obscurity.

Having consulted our botanical colleagues, we have identified a need to contribute to research into conservation and economic botany, but above all for the science of systematics to become a central focus for our work.

SYSTEMATICS

Systematics is the name given to that branch of botany which deals with understanding relationships among plants and which accords to each species a place in a universal classification. It may be thought of as providing the foundation of our understanding of the plant kingdom, by describing differences among its individual member species and then allocating each one its particular place within a universal frame of reference. This branch of botany establishes the current state of knowledge and enables botanists to work within a broad consensus such that all may understand the broad outline of plant diversity in the same way. It is also the branch of botany which occasionally frustrates gardeners and nursery managers by revising plant names. When a plant's name is changed, it is the result of an advance in our scientific knowledge of what distinguishes one species from another. It is not a device to make our lives more complicated, but rather it provides us with a means of understanding complexity more clearly.

The history of plant systematics in the UK is one of the longest and most distinguished in the world. However, the UK Systematics

modern world, this mix allows for a new start, for innovation and unusual partnerships. The Garden, like the new National Assembly for Wales, is embracing sustainability as its guiding principle. We have a detailed policy on sustainable development, which has influenced the design of the Science Centre and the types of experiments that are taking place in the Formal Gardens and on the estate.

Forum and the international programme called Systematics Agenda 2000 (a global strategic plan for systematics) have recently recognised that there is a critical shortage of systematists to document the millions of undescribed species in the world. Only 1.7 million species, out of an estimated 13 million species, have been described so far. Nearly 18 million preserved plant collections from all round the world are held in the UK but there are only 125 botanists, with an average age now exceeding 50 years, to curate them. Few universities teach plant systematics and even fewer recognise botany as a subject. It is, therefore, very significant that Wales is creating a new centre of expertise in systematics at such an important time – a time at which the largest ever extinction of species is taking place in history.

What sort of research, then, is the Garden undertaking to assist the process of maintaining and improving our understanding of those fundamental questions with which the science of systematics concerns itself: What are the earth's species? How are they related? What properties do they have? Where do they occur?

We are concentrating primarily on invasive weeds, horticultural plants, grasses, and fungi. Invasive weeds are now recognised as a major ecological and economic threat to biodiversity. Many of these species are difficult to identify correctly. Using a taxonomic approach, which facilitates scientific identification by establishing definitive descriptions of species, the Garden is researching possible variations within species of invasive weeds in and from temperate, mediterranean and sub-tropical countries. Two early research projects focus on Japanese knotweed (*Fallopia japonica*) and tickberry (*Lantana camara*). Japanese knotweed is particularly bothersome in Wales and is now widespread in Europe and the United States. Tickberry has become one of the greatest threats to species in tropical island systems and to valuable grazing lands in the sub-tropics.

Whilst aggressive weeds pose significant problems to agriculture and to biodiversity in certain endangered habitats, grasses are fundamental to the success of agriculture in a country like Wales, where more land is devoted to livestock production than to the production of crops. Thus, the Garden is developing a long-term study on the taxonomy, evolution and geography of grasses, especially British species and those of agricultural importance to Wales.

Another area of systematics that has been much neglected is the taxonomy of ornamental plants. Many of the major groups of

BELOW *Impenetrable thicket of the invasive species* Lantana camara *(Verbenaceae).*

RIGHT *Tickberry flowers* (Lantana camara) *originated in the West Indies; the species is now widespread throughout the tropics.*

JAPANESE KNOTWEED

Japanese knotweed provides an example of taxonomy as a developing science. In the 1950s the plant belonged to the genus *Polygonum*, which included several species. Japanese knotweed was then accepted to be

RIGHT Fallopia japonica — *Japanese knotweed, invading a car-park wall in Swansea. The species can grow to two metres or more and is very difficult to control.*

P. cuspidatum, and its classification implied a close relationship to other species of *Polygonum*. Later, it was given a revised classification and acquired the new name of *Reynoutria japonica*. This taxonomic review was the result of research which showed that Japanese knotweed belonged to a group of species within the genus *Polygonum* which had more in common with each other than with the defining characteristics of the genus. Further progress has occurred in recent years and, while the plant is still classified in the family Polygonaceae, its genus is now *Fallopia* and its new name is *F. japonica*.

While this may appear as so much splitting of hairs, it is important to be clear about relationships in order to determine control measures in the case of this pernicious weed. Among the tasks which lie ahead is a resolution of the question of whether or not all Japanese knotweed individuals belong to a single species which will respond in a consistent way to control measures. Distinct hybrids occur and confuse the issue. If there is more than one species, or if the species contains variants or sub-species, then account must be taken of that knowledge if effective control is to be devised, particularly biological control of the weed which the Garden supports and will be involved with.

horticulturally important plant genera from temperate and mediterranean regions are in urgent need of taxonomic revision. The Garden is carrying out detailed studies of selected genera. Holders of national collections, horticulturists, gardeners and the trade will benefit from more stable names and clearer species definitions.

There are a number of priority species in the UK Biodiversity Action Plan (see below) which present taxonomic difficulties, especially at the within-species level, or which involve the establishment of new species (e.g. *Senecio cambrensis*) and hybridisation. We are paying particular attention to plants from west Atlantic Europe.

In addition, the Garden is establishing a herbarium of preserved plant and fungal specimens and a library. We will produce a Mycoflora of Wales – an inventory of its fungi, and study the biodiversity of fungi in grasslands and woodlands.

CONSERVATION

We are producing a full inventory of all wild and introduced species visiting or resident on the estate. This inventory allows us to track future changes in the environment that might arise from pollution, new land practices and climate change.

The Garden's conservation programme focuses on the priorities set out in the UK Biodiversity Action Plan. This plan is the UK's response to the Convention on Biological Diversity, and sets out how the UK will map and conserve its fauna and flora and the habitats in which they occur. Special emphasis is placed on the conservation of species of Welsh higher plants, ferns and bryophytes. A collection of rare and endangered Welsh species is being maintained, displayed and interpreted in the Garden. Our first project under this programme is the conservation of *Sorbus leyana* (Ley's whitebeam), which is one of the rarest trees in Britain. This involves protection in the field of the remaining two populations and bulking up plants for re-introduction into the wild.

The Garden is also studying the diversity and dynamics of species of disturbed land, since our knowledge of these is fragmentary. Land use in Wales is undergoing significant change, and so the programme will investigate the impact of changed land use on plant populations and their genetic diversity. Diversification in agriculture could have a significant impact on the pattern and diversity of plants, animals, fungi and landscapes. The programme aims to establish inventories of existing biodiversity in disturbed areas; the surveys reveal potential weed problems, introductions of species from outside the UK, as well as any hybridisation between foreign and indigenous species. The main areas to be surveyed will include road and railway verges, docklands, derelict industrial lands, set-aside lands, and Middleton Hall estate and its surrounds. The latter is important as it builds on the all-species inventory of the estate and will act as a baseline for any escapes of horticultural introductions from the Garden. If livestock farming continues to become uneconomic for family farms in mid- and West Wales, there could be widespread changes in vegetation cover within 10 years. Likewise, the felling of coniferous woodland planted 20–30 years ago will leave acres of disturbed land for colonisation by vegetation or for re-planting with a mix of coniferous and deciduous trees.

As systematics underpins good conservation practice so does an understanding of the breeding systems and ecology of plants. Another area for study is into aspects of flowering and fruiting times, germinability, and fecundity of the introduced and indigenous floras that might be related to global climate change. To this end the Garden is setting up long-term monitoring stations throughout the estate, on small plots that will be used for manipulative experiments (measuring levels of ultraviolet light and carbon dioxide) designed to test a number of contradictory climate-change models. It is important that we are in a position to anticipate and better predict what might happen to the Welsh environment over the next 50–100 years and to establish which of the climate-change models will correctly predict what the countryside will look like and which plants and animals will adapt or die.

The Garden functions as a site for research into fungal ecology, the functional role of fungi in plant survival and growth, and the maintenance of ecosystems. This work is linked to the future development of a centre for the public understanding of fungi at the Garden – a Mycodome, which will be the first of its type in the world.

ABOVE *Bryophytes are a taxonomic group that includes mosses and liverworts, such as* Marchantia polymorpha, *whose spore-forming bodies are shown here (enlarged).*

OPPOSITE *An artist's impression of the Science Centre nestling into the Moorland Hill as seen from the Great Glasshouse.*

ECONOMIC BOTANY

Economic botany is the scientific study of plants that are used by humans. The subject is very varied and embraces diverse uses such as beverages, food, clothing, materials, medicines and cosmetics. In Wales there is considerable interest in increasing agricultural diversification in order to reduce risk and broaden income generation on farms. The Garden is exploring and evaluating a range of potential alternative products: medicinal plants, herbal plants, new ornamentals for landscaping, new biomass crops, and possibly mushroom growing.

We are researching the contemporary and historical use of plants for medicine, a rich tradition dating back over 2,000 years. In line with the majority of British ethnobotanical work conducted abroad in regions rich in biodiversity, this study will be expanded into a European programme for the study of contemporary plant use by Celtic peoples.

THE SCIENCE CENTRE

The planned Science Centre has a distinctive functional design, with transparency and openness as key features. It allows interaction with the public, encourages interdisciplinary research, and provides an open, flexible, innovative and creative working environment. The new building is of high quality and is immersed in one of the Garden's themed landscapes. It comprises three parts: a shared public area, shared laboratories, and private laboratory/office space. In the shared space, visitors can learn about the science being done in the Garden, use the reading room, library resources, and quick-guide herbaria. There are meeting rooms and a special debating area called Plato's Pit, where debates and discussion can take place between the staff and visitors on science

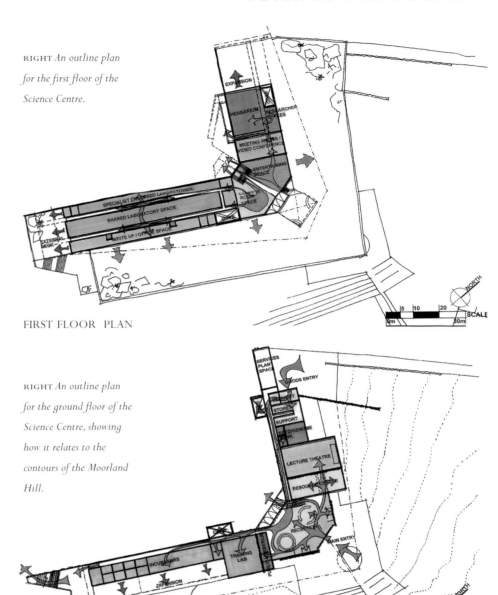

RIGHT An outline plan for the first floor of the Science Centre.

FIRST FLOOR PLAN

RIGHT An outline plan for the ground floor of the Science Centre, showing how it relates to the contours of the Moorland Hill.

GROUND FLOOR PLAN

ABOVE *The Hyder Water Discovery Centre situated on Pwll yr Ardd.*

those of our partners, into commercially viable businesses. Yet we will only allow research to take place that sits comfortably within our own philosophy and ethical positions. All research at the Garden is monitored by our trustees and their advisory groups, who are helping to establish criteria of ethical acceptability.

SCIENCE AND SOCIETY

Our ethos of sustainability and our holistic approach to biological life and its cultural implications has led us to link science to the environmental, educational and horticultural aspirations of the Garden. As our site lies in European Objective 1 region, in which per capita income is less than 75% of the European average, it qualifies for special European regional assistance to raise the standard of living. We therefore have a unique opportunity to contribute to regional regeneration and the improvement of health in Wales.

There is also a broader political context as to why the Garden is embracing science. In the United Kingdom it has long been perceived that, although British scientists are very innovative, they and their institutions are less successful in translating those ideas into improving the lives of people and the environment. With this in mind, the UK Government set up the Technology Foresight programme in 1990 to set clear targets and mechanisms to redress the problem. At the heart of this approach was wealth creation, and an improvement in the quality of personal health and the environment.

THE IMPORTANCE OF COMMUNICATING SCIENCE

The Garden has established links with Welsh research and teaching institutions to pursue common goals, and is collaborating widely with the international scientific community. The emphasis here is on developing new fields of research in Wales which complement the science community, especially plant science, which has a strong base in Wales.

For these links to bear fruit, we must engage the people who need to support the Garden in order to survive themselves. We believe passionately in interacting with the public on the science we carry out. We aim to do this through public debate,

matters. Activities and exhibits within the Centre link to other parts of the Garden, such as the Wallace Garden, which explores genetics, origins of garden plants, and modern genetic controversies. The latter are presented as objectively as possible, giving the arguments both for and against. Also, we are taking care to set out the reasons why the Garden has adopted organic principles. Even though we might adopt certain ethical positions, we will always try to explain why and to present a balanced and factual view to the public so people can make up their own minds.

The Science Centre is designed to enable scientists of different disciplines to interact more with each other. The building is therefore zoned into shared spaces which foster interdisciplinary work. Such work is enhanced by having glass walls separating laboratories from offices. This, with the communal resting and meeting areas, should allow for more opportunities for innovation.

As part of its mission to help generate wealth in the local community the Science Centre houses a special area of offices and laboratories where scientists and biologists can set up new botanical, environmental and education companies. The Garden is the first new garden ever to attempt this. We set out from the start to adopt a more commercial approach, which would encourage the translation of our own science projects, as well as international conferences on the arts–science interface, education programmes, science-based garden exhibits, distance-learning, the Lifelong Learning Centre, outreach work and science festivals. The Science Centre itself is being designed to enable and interest the general public to interact with it through shared resource areas. Science at the National Botanic Garden of Wales is not cut off from the public – visitors will know from day one that we are a scientific institution which aims to make a positive contribution to their lives. There will be a special role for bringing on the next generation of scientists.

The Garden is collaborating with universities and university colleges in the teaching of systematics and other courses. We plan to have post-graduate scientists working at the Garden, and our staff will contribute to the development and delivery of accredited taught and distance-learning post-graduate degrees. Over 40 students have already contributed to scientific research projects on the site since 1996. All our education work will have a strong environmental bias.

The transition to a sustainable society will be more difficult psychologically and politically than it will be economically or technologically, and we need to guard against focusing primarily on the knowledge needed to move to a sustainable society. More fundamentally, we need to help people to develop the will to change the way they and their communities live. If we cannot put the development of humankind and the planet on which we live on a sustainable basis now, then there may not be any further opportunities for such action.

THE SPIRIT OF RIO

At the Garden of Wales our scientific aspirations are linked firmly to the spirit of the Rio Earth Summit, and the need to move from a probable future to a more sustainable and preferred future. We hope that science in the Garden and the way in which we practice it will act as a vehicle to encourage the public to understand and appreciate more deeply the role plants and fungi play in their lives.

At Middleton we have had a rare opportunity to create a new Science Centre from scratch. We have drawn so far on the experiences of many organisations and individuals, but particularly on that of the staff of the new Monsanto Botanical Centre in St Louis (USA), the new Novartis Plant Science Centre (Switzerland), the Welsh School of Architecture in Cardiff (Wales), the National Botanical Institute in Kirstenbosch (South Africa) and the David Leon Partnership (UK). Each of these organisations has shared its experience of building new research centres with us and has helped us avoid costly mistakes. This is what science is all about – building on the work that has gone before in an open, collaborative but rigorous way.

The last few years have been exciting ones. The whole political make-up of Wales has changed since the Garden began to be built. We have learned to live in a more flexible way, to be more focused on our future visitors' needs, to become sensitive to the great changes that are taking place everywhere, and to define our purpose at the beginning of the new millennium. But in the end, although it will be the vision that guides our science, it will be the excitement of new discoveries that will inspire.

SAFE HOUSE

Safe house for barn owl and water-vole,
for natterer's bat and pipistrelle,
for the hairy and the garlic-scented snails,
for Punctum pygmaeum, *the size of a pinhead,*
for adder and dormouse, newt and toad,
for fungi and lichen and the Derwydd daffodil.

The mild western rain of an early spring
will wake the temperate woods of the world,
to the long summer light falling on the Tywi,
on Chinese witchhazel and the snakebark maples,
on strange magnolias and handkerchief trees,
on the monkey puzzle and Chilean flame trees.

Gillian Clarke

GREEN DILEMMAS FOR THE GARDEN

Peter Harper

Being green is a minimum requirement for a major institution of the 21st century, and the National Botanic Garden of Wales has made its commitment very explicit. As the first green botanic garden, it is likely to set environmental standards that will influence other gardens as the new century unfolds. Yet being green is not as straightforward as it first appears, any more for botanic gardens than for households, governments or businesses, which all have to deal with its uncertainties and paradoxes in their own ways.

As far as the National Botanic Garden of Wales is concerned, what other types of organisation have had to face the green question in the past? Who can the Garden look to as an example? Rather than other botanic gardens, it is those self-supporting public demonstration centres that are dedicated to environmental themes and have a strong horticultural dimension. I shall call these places Environmental Visitor Centres or EVCs. I focus on selected examples, and draw on some of them to illustrate the arguments relevant to the Garden at Middleton.

ENVIRONMENTAL VISITOR CENTRES

These are organisations which support themselves from self-generated income, but have a public service ethos focused on environmental values. They actively seek to attract visitors. This allows an intense communication of experience and ideas. Visitor income can also support less public activities. EVCs run their grounds on ecological principles and make serious attempts to practice what they preach. Other features include visitor facilities such as car park, toilets, restaurant, and shop, together with a range of parallel activities such as courses, research, information, publications, service, consultancy, and membership organisations – which may also be income-generating.

Although primarily a botanic garden with a scientific agenda, the National Botanic Garden of Wales shares many of these features, and useful comparisons may be drawn with the following examples.

The Earth Centre is an ambitious environmental demonstration centre opened to the public in 1999, and located on 120 hectares/300 acres of reclaimed colliery spoil near Doncaster. It bears direct comparison with the National Botanic Garden of Wales in that it was made possible by a large Millennium Commission grant, which led to rapid development from a standing start. It aims to attract several hundred thousand visitors a year.

The Centre for Alternative Technology at Machynlleth in mid-Wales was founded in 1974 in a 15-hectare/40-acre slate quarry. It has a broad environmental programme similar to that of the Earth Centre, but has grown 'organically' from small beginnings. Its main income is derived from visitors and sales activities, although it has raised capital through a share issue and

OPPOSITE *The Garden's Great Glasshouse is heated mainly by renewable wood fuel which comes from the Middleton estate.*

POLICIES FOR A GREEN GARDEN

The Garden has laid out its environmental objectives clearly, as shown below:

- Prevent critical and irreversible damage to the environment by anticipating problems rather than responding afterwards.
- Minimise water and energy use through efficient design, management and practice.
- Eliminate the unnecessary use of energy, using renewable energy sources whenever possible.
- Use appropriate energy-efficient or solar-powered, low-level lighting in the landscape.
- Minimise noise (especially from plant and machinery) and odour pollution.
- Minimise polluting effluents and emissions to air.
- Reduce waste through reduction, careful consumption, re-use and recycling. Use organic methods wherever possible.
- Minimise the use of paper and non-recyclable materials. Replace disposables by reusables.
- Assess the environmental impact of all purchases as far as possible in terms of raw materials, manufacture, distribution, use and disposal.
- Avoid use of tropical hardwoods by use of UK-grown hardwoods from sustainable plantations or from the estate.
- Reduce the need for movement both of people and goods and encourage walking, cycling, rail and bus travel wherever practicable. Use sustainable forms of transport on the site wherever possible.
- Reduce the consumption of fossil fuels.
- Manage the buildings and grounds of the site in ways that are environmentally sound and economically sustainable. Assess the aesthetic impact of any new buildings on site.
- Maintain a tidy site with careful storage of all resources.
- Minimise, and where possible eliminate, environmentally damaging substances, materials and processes. Avoid ozone-depleting substances, use biodegradable cleaning materials, and reduce use of volatile organic compounds and materials containing heavy metals.
- Meet and where possible exceed environmental standards, regulations and guidelines.
- Carry out environmental impact assessments of all new developments in the Garden.
- Encourage and promote research on site, and collaborative programmes related to environmental responsibility and sustainable practice.
- Communicate freely the Garden's environmental policy to all.
- Work in partnership with the local community.
- Discourage smoking in all work areas of the Garden by consensus of staff.

other financial initiatives. It has around 80,000 visitors a year, and runs an information service, residential courses, and produces research publications and a quarterly journal.

The Henry Doubleday Research Association at Ryton near Coventry has offered public demonstrations of organic gardening since 1982. It also conducts research with national and international implications, from which it derives a substantial part of its income. It has around 35,000 visitors a year. It also has a 26,000-strong membership organisation and publishes a quarterly journal.

The Eden Project in Cornwall, with its huge greenhouses stretching across a vast china clay quarry, is the EVC most self-consciously styled as a 'theme park'. Although it draws on serious botanical research, it uses entertainment specifically as a vehicle for environmental messages.

De Kleine Aarde (Small Earth) has been in existence since 1972, well known throughout the Netherlands, where it is an influential contributor to the national environmental debate. It receives 20,000 visitors a year and produces organic greenhouse vegetables for the commercial market. It publishes a quarterly journal and many other titles with a strong emphasis on horticulture and food.

Centre Terre Vivante (Living Earth) near Grenoble in France was founded in 1993 as the physical demonstration arm of an organic gardening publishing house. Along with its many book titles, the publishing house produces the very successful bi-monthly *Quatre Saisons du Jardinage*. The grounds were partly designed by Gilles Clément, a contributor to this book.

Environmental policymakers in EVCs face common dilemmas. I shall illustrate these dilemmas by way of three topics: horticultural operations and site management; energy; and catering.

HORTICULTURAL OPERATIONS: ORGANIC STANDARDS FOR PUBLIC GARDENS
In Britain, organic standards for food production – most commonly administered by the Soil Association – are well known; in the Garden's case, organic certification for food products would apply

directly to the operating mixed farm on the estate. The Garden is committed to organic methods wherever possible, but there is as yet no mechanism by which its good practice in amenity horticulture can be externally assessed and certified. Nevertheless, the level of agreement in domestic-scale 'organic gardening' in the UK is fairly good, thanks in large measure to the efforts of the Henry Doubleday Research Association (HDRA), one of our EVC examples. Its series of graded standards provides clear guidance, yet allows gardeners to make pragmatic adjustments according to their circumstances.

Between the legal standards in place for organic food production and the guidelines for amateur gardeners there is a gap where something more formal is needed to cover larger-scale amenity horticulture. The HDRA is currently developing draft guidelines that will almost certainly evolve into a recognised certification system, probably administered by the HDRA itself. The Garden is in a position to make an important practical contribution here, demonstrating imaginative best practice.

The 'normal' organic standards for gardening operate by setting explicit criteria. They have worked for food, and will probably work for landscape and amenity horticulture too. But the non-horticultural aspects of the Garden are too varied and labile for this prescriptive approach. Beyond organic standards, the ISO14000 series offers internationally recognised standards for environmental performance. The key feature is that these standards do not demand high performance at the beginning of an organisation's life span. Rather, they demand an overall plan, regular assessment, complete openness and continual improvement. They encourage a culture of environmental awareness which is seen as a positive asset to the rest of the organisation's functioning. The environmental policy objectives put forward by the Garden make its intentions plain (see opposite). The flexibility allowed by ISO 14001 in the early years will enable the Garden to complete the intensive phase of its development without over-regulation, within a framework which ensures that a softer, greener hand is on the reins when the Garden becomes established, and natural systems have reached their equilibria.

With respect to biodiversity, a cue may be taken from the biologist Jennifer Owen's discovery in her Leicestershire garden

ABOVE *Frogs in a Welsh pond – provide the right habitats and wildlife will adopt them spontaneously.*

that ordinary recreational gardening *automatically* generates innumerable habitats at various scales.

In a conventionally designed, but organically run, garden, she recorded thousands of species, some previously unknown, and was still finding more after 20 years. The moral appears to be that one should simply commit to organic practice and biodiversity will follow. On a larger scale, at the Centre for Alternative Technology (CAT) a total pesticide-free zone has been in operation for 25 years, and toxic paints and timber treatments have been avoided. The overall species count has risen steadily despite intense development and continually increasing human activity. Appropriate management in the National Botanic Garden (which includes, of course, judicious non-management) will almost certainly yield similar results.

A SPRAT TO CATCH A MACKEREL

Whatever policy is adopted in day-to-day horticultural operations, the environmental impact of any policy is likely to be negligible when compared with the impact of the visitors to the Garden and the facilities they require. The more successful the Garden becomes, the more visitors will arrive, demanding more car parks, toilets, paths, seats, restaurants, sales points and souvenirs. How do we apply green yardsticks here? It is not logical to condemn growth as such, since we must assume that the existence of the institution as a visitor centre is on balance positive. We are really talking about the ratio between the necessary environmental impact of an organisation and its success in achieving or stimulating environmental improvements. This is the 'sprat to catch a mackerel' principle, which applies to all such organisations: little sprat, big mackerel – relatively speaking. There is nearly always scope for reducing the size of the sprat, releasing resources to catch more mackerel. On the other hand, the very act of measurement can raise a number of imponderables.

ENERGY: THE GARDEN AND BEYOND

One factor which is fairly easy to measure and is often a good proxy for wider environmental impact is energy. Energy use and its implications probably share top billing with biodiversity in questions of sustainability. Some statistics from CAT show what is a typical pattern. Energy used in horticultural operations is so small as to be virtually unmeasurable. The main identifiable categories are:

- Heating for buildings, hot water and cooking: 2,020 gigajoules (GJ) (77%)
- Electricity for all usual purposes: 307 GJ (11%)
- Transport for commuting, business trips, local freight: 313 GJ (12%).

Total: 2,640 GJ (1998 figures).

It is difficult to calculate how 'good' this is, because it is not clear whether an EVC should compare its energy consumption with that of a house, a factory, or an office. Should the ratio be calculated per employee, per visitor or per unit of turnover? The equation becomes even more complex if energy generated from renewable sources is calculated differently from that which is not. Finally, energy saved through efficiency and conservation measures defies accurate assessment without a baseline for comparison.

These difficult questions of operational energy use are put firmly in perspective by looking at the energy used by visitors to travel to the site. It is one of the bitterest discoveries of any EVC that it is utterly dependent on the private motor car. The Earth Centre, for example, has a railway station right on its doorstep, but very few visitors use it. At CAT, in spite of fairly good public transport links, over 95% of visitors come by car. Most are 'tourists' already in the area, making trip lengths of about 50 miles with an average occupancy of 3. With typical fuel economy, this would use about 4,000 GJ of primary energy per annum. Ironically, even more energy is consumed by the minority of 'green pilgrims' who have

travelled specially to visit the site, with an average trip length of 300 miles and average car occupancy of 2 – around 9,000 GJ per annum. The total of 13,000 GJ needed just to get the visitors to the site is nearly five times the total operating energy of CAT, not to mention the other environmental impacts caused by all this traffic. This ratio is similar for the Henry Doubleday Research Association, and is likely to be worse for the Earth Centre and for the National Botanic Garden of Wales, both of which have far higher anticipated visitor numbers.

LEFT *A blot on the Welsh landscape? This 600-kilowatt wind generator at CAT saves as much fossil fuel as visitors use in travelling to see it.*

One of the implications of this understanding is that reducing operational energy no longer has much absolute significance, but is undertaken as a demonstration, or to save money. In absolute terms, attention must shift to the visitor transport, which ironically arises from the very success of the project. Is it completely beyond the control of an EVC? Several responses to this dilemma have been considered, each with its own philosophical luggage. One is to spend more effort strengthening public transport links, but these cannot be directly controlled by the Garden.

Another approach is to accentuate the price differences between cars and other modes of transport. It is logical to charge for car parking, and the Earth Centre did just this, on a per head basis. There were, however, bitter complaints that this approach penalised those who had deliberately filled up a car to passenger capacity for the journey, and now the Earth Centre operates a flat charge. Another EVC provides free parking but gives a 20% discount for holders of rail or bus tickets and a 50% discount for cyclists and pedestrians. These are largely symbolic gestures with little discernible impact on visitors' transport choices or the organisation's income. On this account, perhaps the opportunity should be taken for more conspicuous initiatives that could be widely advertised, for example, 'Car-Free? – Entry Free': the word would soon get

about that 'X lets you in free if you don't go by car'. Accountants might worry about a loss of income here, but experience suggests that visitors who feel they have saved money on the entrance fee are inclined to spend it on other things on the site.

Another approach is purely conceptual. We simply ask: can we measure the environmental impact of running the EVC against its redeeming benefits? At CAT, the energy cost per visitor amounts to about 0.15 GJ. This is small in relation to a typical household's annual energy consumption of 100–200 GJ, and the organisation might reasonably expect to have at least this much influence on its visitors' energy awareness and consumption. If so, we can claim that the energy consumption caused as a result of the EVC's existence is indeed a sprat to catch a mackerel.

A third approach would be to mitigate the effects of visitor transport by (for example) planting trees to absorb CO_2. One could imagine a car park fee being described as a 'carbon surcharge' destined for energy saving or tree planting, not necessarily on the EVC site. In some centres there might be scope for tree-planting by visitors, complete with a ruddy-cheeked 'feel-good' factor.

Generating renewable energy beyond the operational needs of the site is another 'mitigating' strategy. A wind generator or water turbine that feeds directly into the National Grid displaces the use of fossil fuels and it is not unrealistic to consider supplying more energy than is used by visitors in getting to the Garden in this way.

EATING GREEN

The grand energy picture gives us some idea of what we might have to do to reduce the *actual* total impact of the operation's activity. Another invariable feature of a visitor centre is the Restaurant, and here we run up against what we might call the *virtual*: what its visitors think. An *actually* green restaurant might have to make assessments in many different directions: the kind of food it sells, the way this food is prepared, the crockery and cleaning materials used, the recycling of food wastes, waste water treatment, staff working conditions and so on. Some of these assessments are easy to make, but most are paradoxical. Perhaps the greatest paradox is that the restaurant could potentially do more for the green cause through its influence on customers than

BELOW *The greatest paradox of any EVC is that its success is proportional to the number of car trips made by visitors.*

through being thoroughly but invisibly green. But this itself is a delicate matter. For example, should the type of food available in a green restaurant aim at a 'globally sustainable diet', say one with very little meat, based mostly on local, organically produced food? Or should it be based on a 'healthy diet' (whole ingredients, no additives, low fat, lots of fresh vegetables)? And how would such messages come across?

Take the example of plates and cups. The three materials commonly used in making cups are ceramics, paper, and plastic/styrofoam. Ceramics are associated with 'a better class of restaurant' and the other materials with cheaper cafeterias. No EVC would be seen dead with disposable materials (see the Garden's environmental objectives, on page 134). It might seem obvious that reusable ceramics are superior environmentally, particularly on energy grounds, while paper might be thought marginally better than styrofoam. In energy terms however, it is actually the other way round. The life-cycle energy cost of making, delivering, washing and drying a ceramic cup over its typical life (say, 200 cycles) is actually greater than making, delivering and disposing of an equivalent number of styrofoam cups. This is due largely to the hot water required for cleaning, and the need to treat the resultant dirty water. Styrofoam is also preferable to disposable paper in energy terms, although if the paper is composted (as it should be) the gap narrows.

This is all very surprising, and might even drive a green catering manager to dig up more dirt on styrofoam in order avoid the appalling conclusion that being green demands a switch from ceramics to plastic. More litter, surely, with plastics; more space taken up in landfill; dioxins from incineration; babies choking. Indeed, but how do we weigh these against energy issues, which originally we were happy to use as a stick to beat plastic? More likely the choice will be made simply on what *seems* most green. The average visitor will not be aware of these life-cycle calculations and would be baffled and confused by the existence of styrofoam cups in a quality restaurant. This is extremely important for EVCs. The influence of green clichés is pervasive. Visitors will often expect certain things and feel disappointed, even swindled, if they do not find them. Many have paid good money to have their ideals massaged. Decision-making is fraught with problems, even for experienced eco-analysts. Sound practice in terms of one objective, like energy, might represent bad practice in relation to another, such as pollution or aesthetics.

COMPULSORY ORGANIC?

While we are still in the restaurant, we should ask ourselves whether an EVC should provide organic food. Again, it might seem obvious that it should, but this can lead to yet another set of dilemmas. Organic food of the appropriate range and quality is not always easily available, and is often very expensive. This puts up restaurant operating costs and the customer may well have to meet those costs. If customers are not given a choice between organic and cheaper alternatives, they may be unhappy about being forced to pay higher prices. When trying to communicate with visitors who might be unfamiliar with green ideas, vegetarian and 'wholefood' (freshly prepared from raw ingredients) represent the nutritional end of traditional greenness. But, if the communication is to be effective, it is important not to alienate customers by high-priced and 'inaccessible' food.

GETTING THROUGH THE MINEFIELD

It should be clear from the above that, alas, the process of 'greening' is a philosophical minefield. What are we to do? The metaphor itself suggests a curious analogy: it was said of Russian troops during the Second World War that they never tried to clear minefields but simply marched through them, hoping for the best and accepting the consequences. They lost fewer men with this robust approach than they would have through the Western alternative of step-by-step clearance which, aiming for zero casualties, slowed an advance and exposed the troops to enemy fire. Perhaps EVCs have a similar choice. Aiming for a perfect and consistent environmental policy slows us to a standstill and leaves us exposed to withering fire from critics within and without, not to mention the harsh winds of commercial reality. Even then we might end up tangled in paradoxes and back where we started. Perhaps, in the short term at least, we have to adopt a robust and pragmatic 'Russian' approach to environmental minefields — just get on with things and make the best decisions we can, with a genuine commitment to constant improvement. It is probably the only sane way.

THE SOCIAL ECOLOGY OF THE GARDEN

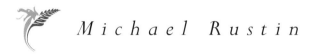

Michael Rustin

This chapter will explore the idea that the concept of ecosystem, an environment consisting of a community of interacting organisms, can be illuminating in a more than botanical or biological sense. It is a powerful metaphor for social and cultural links, and can help us to understand the National Botanical Garden of Wales as an element in a wider social and cultural context.

At its simplest, a botanic garden is a collection of growing plants, displayed for the enjoyment and education of the public. The displays, so much more spacious and abundant than most gardeners can create, give pleasure for their beauty, and arouse interest and wonderment for their variety and complexity. Traditionally, botanic gardens reflected botanists' scientific interest in the naming and classification of plants. For many lay visitors, what distinguished a botanic garden from a beautiful park was the array of name tags on the plants, and the visual instruction to visitors on the characteristics of the different plant species. These gardens, often attached to universities, were a public display and record of the work of botanists engaged worldwide in the discovery, retrieval, collection and taxonomy of plants. In Britain, the great botanic gardens have been one of the most benign outcomes of the explorations associated with the British Empire – the botanist in his search for specimens, like the zoologist, the archaeologist, and the anthropologist, usually following the colonisers.

Scientific interests in nature have long moved beyond taxonomy, seeking better to understand nature as a system. Habitats, not the individual plant species within them, have received increasing attention. The dependence of plants on particular geological and climatic environments, the interdependence of species upon one another, their relation to animal species and human activities, and their 'succession' (their occupation of habitats over periods of time) have become major topics for investigation. Botanic gardens have been adapted to reflect these new preoccupations; plants are arrayed in small-scale reproductions of their natural environments – for example, deserts, alpine conditions, acid soils – and in re-creations of their geographical locations of origin. The National Botanic Garden of Wales will fully reflect and illustrate this 'ecological' frame of reference.

The development and popularisation of the neo-Darwinian paradigm, explaining the conditions for evolutionary success of different species in relation to one another, has been a prominent feature of the intellectual landscape of recent years. Evolutionists like Richard Dawkins and Stephen Jay Gould have become best-selling authors, and numerous television series, such as David Attenborough's *The Life of Plants*, have exposed mass audiences to neo-Darwinian explanations of how different species come to be what they are, where they are, and for what reasons.

ABOVE *The open vents of the Great Glasshouse — connecting inner and outer worlds — ideas and information, as well as atmospheric gases, are exchanged in the Garden.*

The National Botanic Garden of Wales seeks to inform its visitors in many ways about the properties of habitats, and their relations with topography, climate, human interventions, colonisations, invasions, and pollutants. Human interventions which were once implicitly or explicitly celebrated in the displays of botanic gardens are now topics for critical study and public warning. Botanic gardens have become centres of conservation – sometimes of actual or potential re-colonisation – where once they were the focus of collections from environments then in little danger from human activity.

The concept of ecology, which is the study of the relationships between living things, is fundamental to what botanic gardens study and display, but it may also be applied beyond botany and biological science. We now understand 'natural' ecosystems as being usually by no means 'natural'. Most plant environments in the world, and virtually all of them in the British Isles, are the outcome of interactions between the natural environment and human activities. What is enjoyed by many as the most 'wild' area of the British Isles, the Highlands of Scotland, is in fact the product of forest clearances, the expulsion of cultivators from the land, and the replacement of crofting by sheep-grazing, over two or three centuries. The uplands of Wales, to which we seek free access to experience a sense of wilderness and the cry of the kite, are artefacts, produced initially

by centuries of 'transhumance', which is when stock are taken out of the valleys to graze the hillsides in summer. Conservation of the present landscape may be threatened or assisted by contemporary trends in land use, and some would argue that the use of Highland moors for game-shooting represents the most secure form of custodial input available for these remote tracts. We need social equivalents of the idea of 'ecosystem' to understand nature, and the plant world within it.

The National Botanic Garden of Wales reproduces and displays many natural ecosystems. But it is a work of human design too, and has shaped its representations of nature in accordance with current scientific knowledge. The Garden will thus be a new point of connection between nature and culture. It will generate new understandings of these links through its own work. In addition, the idea of ecosystem has a wider application, in relation to the Garden, than to nature alone. The Garden is a 'node' or growing-point in a variety of systems, and not only biological ones. Such social and cultural ecosystems will intersect with the Garden's primary work of cultivation, investigation and education in many different and unpredictable ways.

Consider the dimensions of the socio-cultural ecosystems on which the National Botanic Garden of Wales depends. At its core, as its germinating seed or 'meme', was the idea itself that there should be a National Botanic Garden of Wales ('In the beginning was the Word…'). But ideas are also components of systems, linked to other ideas. The idea of a National Botanic Garden of Wales at this point in history presupposes, and will add meaning to, the idea that Wales is a nation, something that might have been open to doubt some twenty years ago. But it is because the Garden has taken the stage as a major new national institution in Wales that generous funding streams, from government and other sponsors, have been diverted to its creation.

A botanic garden is most obviously a scientific institution, which needs credibility in the scientific world, links with universities, and activities of research and scholarship. The appointment as its Director of a scientist who was previously Deputy Director at the Royal Botanic Gardens at Kew firmly establishes the Garden's standing within this scientific network. The Garden has planned its specialist inputs into botanical science. The standing and relevance of a botanic garden also depends on visitors. Although its location is relatively remote, it is close to the M4 and the A40, the main roads from southern England and South Wales to Holyhead and Ireland. This is a locational benefit – in fact a necessity for a successful public garden. Millions of people will drive close by the Garden entrance, especially in the summer months, and may be persuaded to visit it during their journey. But this proximity also involves a risk, that the Garden may be swamped by a variety of visitors more interested in the facilities of a motorway stopover than in the special qualities of a botanic garden. The challenge is to interact with the different levels of interest and expectation among the Garden's visitors, and to leave them all with a deeper sense of enjoyment of plants, and of their value to humanity.

The Garden from its inception has been establishing networks and links of various other kinds. The decision to invite Norman Foster to design the Great Glasshouse immediately established the Garden as a major centre of interest in the world of architecture. The choice of the eminent landscape designers engaged in the project link it to another professional and artistic field. The incorporation of the qualities and associations of the previous site express an aesthetic commitment to conservation and continuity which will be meaningful and important to those interested in Welsh history and locality. The decision to construct the Garden on an environmentally 'self-sustaining' basis, by using and displaying systems of recycling and energy conservation, links the Garden to those committed to environmental protection, and makes it a potential exemplar or showcase for the green movement. The commitment to feature traditional medicinal plants as an element in the Garden both reconnects it to the earliest botanic gardens – physic gardens – but also to ancient Welsh folk medicine, as well

LEFT *Plant names displayed in a botanic garden – the Chelsea Physic Garden.*

ABOVE *The Witch Hazel,* Hamamelis mollis, *is a popular winter-flowering shrub introduced to Britain from China in 1879.*

as to contemporary 'alternative medicine'. The Fire, Earth, Water and Air themes underlying the Garden's design link it back in time, to the origins of science and philosophy. The conjunction of current scientific investigation with the rediscovery (no doubt in part the reinvention) of pre-scientific traditions of many kinds makes the Garden paradoxically more 'up-to-date' and in touch with contemporary culture than if it had opted for a more 'purist' and one-dimensional scientific identity.

Plans to engage artists in the work of the Garden connect with another stream of activity and interest. Plants and landscapes have always been a major inspiration and field of representation for visual artists, and the illustration of plants has provided a practical link between art and botany. Whereas in the past institutions devoted to science have tended to insist on their distance from the merely expressive or imaginative realms, the National Botanic Garden of Wales seems to be committed to their re-connection, and to a new kind of cultural hybridisation of science with the arts. The engagement of artists in the work of the Garden could take many forms, from the use of its sites as exhibition spaces, to the specific cultivation and study of the arts most related to landscape and nature.

In recent years photography and film have been a vital resource for originating and disseminating botanical knowledge (through microscopic and time-lapse photography, for example). Many people now learn much of what they know about plants (and other elements of the natural world) through film and photograph, especially through television. Who can forget David Attenborough's insect-eating plants, clinging to rocks and deluged by water, evolved to attract insects as their food because there are no other nutrients available to them? The Bioverse section of the Garden extends this type of visual access to nature. Outside opening hours, and regardless of the constraints of local time, 'virtual' visitors from all over the world may access the Garden's website, leading them one day perhaps to visit Middleton in person.

There are 'economies of scale' to be achieved by the conjunction of these multifarious activities, each of them 'exploiting' the Garden's primary commitment to the culture of plants and plant communities in different ways. There is bound, for example, to be a 'rainy day problem' for a Garden situated in West Wales. Art and film will provide ways of enjoying, and being informed by, the

Garden, even when its outdoor attractions are diminished by downpour, mud, and monochrome skies. The Great Glasshouse and indoor display sites will maintain visitors' confidence that it will be worth setting out for the Garden even when the weather cannot be relied upon.

Middleton is located in a region which has rather few competitive economic activities, and relatively little tourism. There is opportunity for it to become a stimulus to regional regeneration, since the attention of visitors attracted by the Garden will 'spill over' into adjacent attractions. A national botanic garden will become, whether it likes it or not, a key part of the Welsh tourist industry. Together with the nearby Newton House and Dinefwr Park, the fine castles of the Tywi Valley, and the 'garden lost in time' of Aberglasney, the National Botanic Garden is capable of redefining and strengthening the cultural heritage of Carmarthenshire.

Thus this Garden is not only a garden of plants, but also a centre for scientific research and education. Its architecture and its bio-system engineering will attract interest in their own right. It will gather and renew cultural traditions – some of them related to Welsh culture and heritage, and some of them connected with much wider concerns for the environment. As a significant innovation in the economy of West Wales, it will attract more

OPPOSITE The kitchen garden at Aberglasney, recently restored and close to the National Botanic Garden of Wales.

BELOW A corner of the Pool Garden at Aberglasney – overlooked by the terrace outside Gardener's Cottage, which abuts an 'enigmatic cloister range'.

OPPOSITE *Llanstephan Castle at the mouth of the river Tywi, a little over 20 kilometres of 'Dylan Thomas country' from the Garden — as the crow flies.*

LEFT *Three Cliffs Bay on the Gower peninsula — the natural heritage of the South Wales coast.*

people and more trade to the area. And as a centre for the display, and perhaps the production, of art, it will chart new cultural waters. As Raymond Williams pointed out in his book *The Country and The City*, the concept of 'culture' derived its primary meaning from the idea of the culture of plants, and it is from this that the broader notion of human culture emerged.

How can we explain the way in which a botanic garden can appear to be so many things, and have so many functions, all at once? How do we explain why it actually needs to be so many things, to succeed in its primary role as a Garden? The idea of ecosystem is one way of understanding this, if we broaden this idea to include not only the botanical inputs and outputs of water, light, nutrients, seed, and dead matter, but also the other inputs of an economic, intellectual and social kind, which sustain the Garden as an organisation, a laboratory, and a centre of culture.

Another illuminating way of thinking about the Garden is through what is called 'Actor–Network Theory'. This is a body of ideas developed by the French sociologist of science, Bruno Latour, and his colleagues in France and Britain. They set out to explain how scientific ideas succeed or fail in their competitive environment – their particular 'ecosystem'. Scientists succeed in propagating their ideas (or fail to do so) by establishing alliances through which research funds, reputations, and applications are achieved. Latour's *The Pasteurisation of France* is a brilliant study of Pasteur's discovery of bacilli. It shows that what was real in the laboratory only became real in practical terms, on farms and in hospitals, when farmers, doctors and governments were persuaded to take discoveries of the bacilli seriously. They had to create conditions outside the lab in which the effects of the invisible pathogens,

THE SOCIAL NETWORK

The opening of the National Botanic Garden of Wales is only the start of a process; its sustenance and growth depends on continuing flows and transactions with a social and cultural environment. These flows and transactions require that we see the Garden as a site of 'production', and not merely as a place of consumption and display to which people come to enjoy and learn about plants. What is going to be 'produced' is not only plants, but also includes:

- new scientific ideas
- aesthetic experiences
- educational outputs and events
- regenerated local traditions
- a renewal of folk medicine
- contributions to ecological thinking
- a strengthening of Welsh national identity
- tourists and trade for bed and breakfast providers, pubs, and hotels
- customers for garden centres, near and far
- sales of plants and books on site and on line
- exhibition space, and new networks, for artists
- educational opportunities for Welsh schools
- international links with other botanical gardens
- lifelong learning opportunities
- revolving audio-visual theatre and exhibition

RIGHT *Walking around the flow of the rill, as it spirals into the centre of the Circle of Decision on The Broadwalk.*

and of the vaccines deployed against them, could be observed and tested.

The links through which such alliances are achieved are often conceptual or metaphorical. For example, in Darwin's great work on evolution, the idea of selective breeding became extended from the deliberate breeding of species to obtain the improved qualities wanted by farmers or gardeners, to the idea of random variations occurring in nature, which could confer selective advantage through the competitive struggle for survival. This idea of the selective evolutionary advantage that can arise from mutation then became extended in its turn to the sphere of society, and became a popular metaphor for life seen as a competitive struggle.

The idea of ecosystem is in some ways the converse of this idea, stressing not competition but interdependency, and the ways in which the properties of a whole system can sustain each part of it. The botanical ecosystems created in the Garden, thus serve to display in microcosm the wider ecosystems of nature. In many ways, for example through its methods of recycling, the Garden encourages its visitors to reflect on the complex interdependencies not only within nature, but within the relations between mankind and the natural world. The idea of wider social ecosystems enables us to recognise that the Garden exists in intellectual, economic and political spaces, as well as in a botanical space. The Garden has to take these environments seriously in order to survive and grow.

Thus from the initial idea for the National Botanic Garden of Wales, alliances had to be established and support won in order for the Garden to become a reality. This happened through many different, intersecting networks of ideas and social relations. Wales was again becoming perceived to be a 'nation'. It seemed reasonable to suggest that a national botanic garden was what a 'nation' might appropriately have, for cultural, scientific and environmentalist reasons. Gardens have been important in recent years in providing low-cost 'kick-starts' to processes of renewal, more often through the garden festivals of Glasgow, Liverpool and Ebbw Vale than in the deepest countryside. But these garden festivals were short-lived affairs. A botanic garden is a permanent feature (though without cultivation, it would not last long), feasible on low-cost land, and capable of catalysing regional regeneration in a slow-acting but longer-lasting way.

UPPER CARBONIFEROUS

From Abercarn, Gwent, from the tropical swamp
that made the coal your fathers cut.
When they were boys down the deep shaft
in darkness swept by a lamp,
they'd ache at the breath of bluebells brought
by a May wind in the downdraft,
for the woods and the sunlight,
they'd miss that shift.

Gillian Clarke

Numerous personal and social linkages will have been indispensable to this foundation.

In short, the National Botanic Garden of Wales is the social and cultural equivalent of a large new ecosystem, planted in an area with a previously low density of activity. It will interact in vigorous and multifarious ways with a whole host of other 'environments', both near and at a distance.

It is not easy for institutions to manage such complexity. The Garden, committed to 'biodiversity', will need to develop the internal organisational equivalent of this variety to work productively. A monocultural style, which lays down that the Garden is only about science, or visitor flows, or only about Welsh identity, could be as limiting as the monoculture of plants, and would prevent the realisation of the full potential of the Garden. The Garden's potential lies in all the possible interactions and cross-fertilisations between different elements of its project. By recognising its own necessary complexity, as a community of co-existent 'organisms', it will increase its relevance and influence. In this way the National Botanic Garden of Wales can bring back to the world of public institutions a recognition of complexity and interdependence which it gains from its understanding of nature.

N A T
A N D   F U

U R E
T U R E

THE GARDEN IN NATURE

Kate Soper

The National Botanic Garden of Wales testifies to our pleasure and interest in nature, and provides a unique opportunity for reflecting upon its significance in our lives. Yet the Garden is also coming into being at a time of very intensive discussion and controversy about the nature of 'nature' and even about its continued existence.

There is much talk today about the 'end' or 'disappearance' of nature, where what is meant is that there is little or nothing of the environment that remains unaffected by human activity; and little studied in botany and biology that is not subject to human manipulation. Nature, we are told, has now itself become the 'construct' of human culture: an argument which often carries the suggestion that, as we have 'constructed' it, so we have brought about the destruction of its authentic or pristine form.

In presenting humanity and its works as antithetical to those of nature, such claims invite us to think that human culture is external to, or set apart from, the natural order. Yet clearly we are also in some sense 'natural' animals who have biological features and ecological dependencies akin to those of other living creatures. So we have to ask in what this separation consists – and in pondering this, we are in turn led on to further questions about what counts as nature, and why.

What are the differences between what human beings are, do and make, and the being and doing of other creatures? Why, for example, is the ant heap or beehive seen to belong to the natural

environment, whereas even the most primitive of human dwellings is looked upon as an artificial excrescence? What is it exactly that makes us think of some parts of the environment as more natural than others? Is the city of Swansea, for example, less a part of the natural order than the National Botanic Garden of Wales, or the latter less so than its surrounding countryside – and, if so, why? What is the difference between the beauty or value of a work of art and that of a beautiful aspect of nature (a landscape, a flower, a bird)? Why do we think of the 'real' tree or flower as both more natural – and more beautiful – than the artificial even though the 'real' plant may be just as much the product of human design (through breeding or training) as the fabricated flower?

In short, what boundaries do we want to observe – and why – between the organic and inorganic, between the human and the animal, between art, artifice and nature – and how do the answers we give to these questions bear on our current ecological concerns about what we are doing to nature, and it to us?

PERENNIAL QUESTIONS, PARTICULAR ANXIETIES

At the beginning of the third millennium, these issues are among the most hotly contested in Western societies. Yet some of the questions around which the current debate revolves – and some, too, of the reflections offered in response to them – have a long

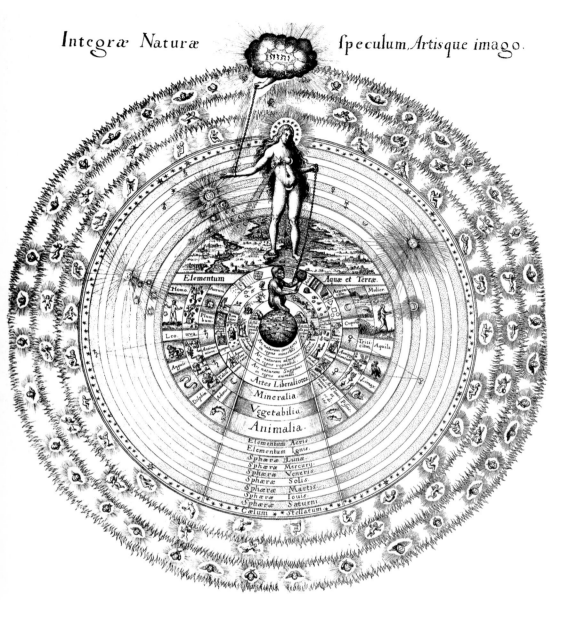

Integræ Naturæ Speculum, Artisque imago.

of maintaining biodiversity and the unpredictable consequences of any subtraction, however minor, from the ecosystem. In line, moreover, with the overall conception of the Chain, we are asked today to view nature, not as an external context, but as an integral whole within which each being has its particular function and purpose in maintaining the whole.

But despite some striking similarities with the situation we find ourselves in today, there are important differences. Even though Western culture has continuously debated the nature of 'nature' and the human role within it, the historical context of this debate has changed so dramatically that every epoch must be said to live out a quite particular set of interests and anxieties in its questionings.

In the Middle Ages, the central concerns were religious: they were about God's power and purposes in creating the universe, and whether humans had been granted a licence by Him to exploit all earthly resources in their own interests, or been entrusted with the more pastoral task of acting as stewards of its plant and animal kingdom. Nature itself, in this period, was viewed as having mysterious and magical powers and was regarded with awe and superstition.

In the course of the scientific revolution of the 17th and 18th centuries, this perspective gradually yielded to the idea that nature could be objectively known, and manipulated, by the rational and self-motivating powers which Humanist and Enlightenment philosophers claimed for the human individual. Freedom was held to depend on the realisation of human powers previously held in thrall to superstitious conceptions of the natural world and to theological bigotries about its divine ordination. But this Enlightenment confidence also went together with unprecedented industrialisation, human exploitation and environmental degradation – and these developments were in turn countered by the Romantic concern over the 'loss' of nature, and its call to return to nature as a source of human redemption.

This tension has persisted into our own times, where we are still living out the contradiction between the pressures for economic growth and technological expansion, on the one hand, and those for a sustainable economy, global justice and environmental protection, on the other – and it is this which gives

ABOVE *'The Mirror of Nature as totality and image of Art'. Nature is conceived as an integral work of creation in this English School 18th-century engraving.*

history, and in their essentials have remained quite similar across the ages. For instance, the ongoing concerns with the 'totality' of nature and the human place within it are embedded in current thinking on the organic integration of the planetary ecosystem, but were also at the root of early Christian teaching about the Great Chain of Being. Conceived as linking all entities from the lowest to the highest in relations of such close dependency that chaos would ensue were any 'link' to be struck out, the idea of the Chain finds an echo in contemporary arguments about the importance

ABOVE *Jan Bruegel and Peter Paul Rubens' 'The Sense of Smell': the garden is used allegorically in one of several collaborations between the two painters. Bruegel painted the flowers and Rubens the figures.*

particular quality and urgency to our current questionings about nature. Today the debate reflects both our ecological anxieties about pollution, resource distribution and depletion, and our doubts, and fears, about what still counts as 'nature' in a world so technically controlled and made over by human beings.

CULTURE AND NATURE 2000

As we have seen, one way in which these concerns are reflected in current thinking about the nature of 'nature' is through an emphasis on the inclusion of humanity within an order of nature viewed, as in the Gaia perspective, as holistic ecosystem. Yet even if we allow that all living beings exist in the largest sense in some kind of integral whole, we must still recognise that without humanity there would be no concept of 'nature' in the first place, no distinction between the 'natural' and the 'cultural', and none of the discriminations we have noted between nature and artifice or art. Human beings, moreover, are able consciously to monitor and, in principle, adjust their impact on the environment in ways denied to other creatures. So even though we see ourselves as broadly part of the order of nature, there are also grounds to emphasise our distinctness within it, and even, in some respects, our separation from it.

Indeed, environmentalists often present themselves as seeking to preserve nature from human intrusion or contamination. The 'eco-warriors' protesting against road and airport extension, for example, see themselves, or at any rate are depicted by the media, as locked in a battle for the protection of 'nature' against the further encroachments of the 'human'. From this perspective, nature has 'intrinsic value': it is an independent good worth cherishing in itself, and not simply as a source of raw materials available for human use.

But compelling as it is in many ways, the demand to respect nature in this way does tend to imply that there is a hard and fast distinction to be drawn between what is given in nature and what is done by human beings, and this can be a problem. If, for example, we think of 'nature' as that which is wholly independent of, and unaffected by, humanity, then it is clear that very little of what we loosely think of as the 'natural' environment — field systems, downlands, woodlands and wetlands and their flora and fauna — can qualify for the term. Even 'Wild Wales' is for the most part a culturally modified landscape bearing the imprint of centuries of human habitation and management.

Today we value the wilder parts of the environment precisely because of their remoteness and their relative freedom from the

BELOW *Hans Wertinger, 'Summer'. An image of cultivated nature. The natural environment is here depicted as provider of resources and place of human recreation.*

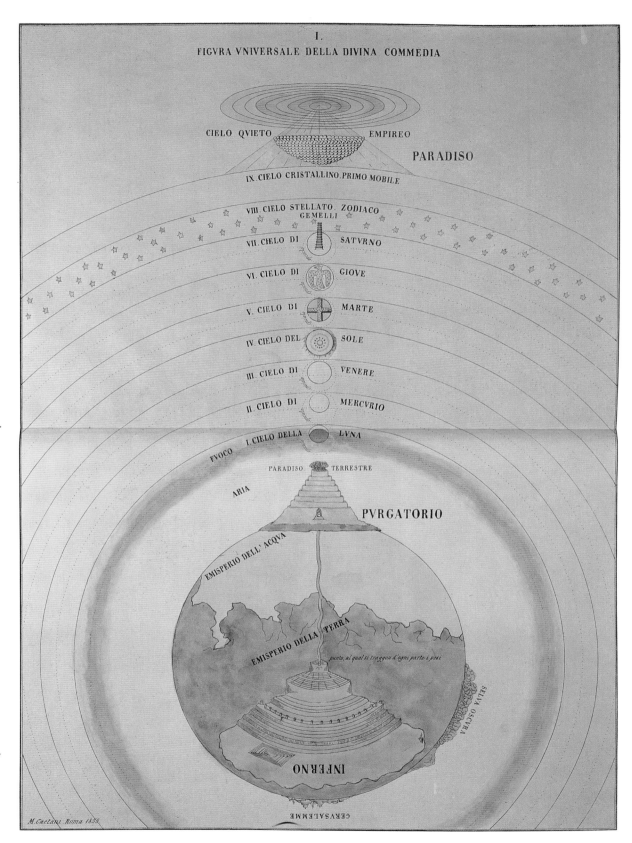

RIGHT *The world as conceived by the poet Dante, c. 1300, from an 1872 study by Michelangelo Caetani. It combines the Christian vision of Heaven, Purgatory and Hell with the Aristotelian concept of the spheres.*

RIGHT *'Vase of Flowers'*,
by Ambrosius Bosschaert.
Dutch, late 16th century.
This is an image from late
Humanist culture which
reveals an intense interest
and delight in the detail
and differentiation of
natural objects.

impact of human industry. But this has not always been the case. Tastes in landscape and the favoured forms for country estates and gardens have themselves changed considerably over time and reflect responses to industrial activity. The mountainous regions and rugged landscapes that we much admire today for their 'sublimity' were in the Middle Ages regarded as distressing legacies of the Flood or thought of as ugly and inhospitable. If the once more frightful parts of the environment have now become appealing in their very wildness, this arguably testifies to the extent to which fears of nature have been overcome in the course of its scientific subjugation and domestication. What counts, moreover, as being beautiful or as having intrinsic value in nature is conditioned by economic and social factors that are in turn further mediated through their representation in art, literature, and other forms of nature imagery. In other words, what we define and value as the 'difference' or 'otherness' of nature is itself culturally formed.

To complicate matters further, technological developments in recent times have blurred the line between the natural and the cultural. Some have argued that the computer with its mechanical extensions of mind and memory and its creation of virtual realities, is making redundant any distinction between the organic and the inorganic, and that we should think of ourselves increasingly as 'cyborg' entities, part machine-like, part organic. Innovations in medicine and genetic engineering have been cited to similar effect. Prosthetic enhancements such as heart pacers and other sophisticated replacements of human body parts, gene therapy, cloning, genetically modified seeds and foods, the creation of transgenic entities such as Astrid the Pig or OncoMouse: all this, it is said, serves to render ever more fuzzy the distinctions between the human, the animal and the machine-like. These 'advances' also indicate the extent to which what is natural in the sense of being alive and organic has itself been transformed by, even become the 'construct' of, humanly contrived technologies.

ETHICAL DILEMMAS

Amidst this plethora of accounts of nature and of the human role both in its destruction and construction, it can be difficult to find one's bearings. One thing, however, does seem clear: it is only because we do (and arguably cannot but) observe distinctions between the human, the animal, the biotic and the inorganic, that we experience the ethical concerns we do about the future of nature. If we were no longer to notice these differences then neither Dolly the Sheep, nor OncoMouse, nor the prospect of human cloning, nor artificial brain implants, nor any of the current sources of alarm about 'Frankenstein' science would cause us any grief. So those who recommend we overcome our commitments to these 'outdated' divides may be undermining the bases of moral concerns whether for human rights or for the preservation of nature.

What also seems clear is that none of the arguments about the 'disappearance' or the 'construction' of nature can dispense with a distinction between the 'nature' which human beings do not and cannot create and the 'nature' which is the consequence of their interventions. Even the most sophisticated experiments in genetic modification work with, and are dependent for their success upon, pre-given biological laws and processes. In this sense there is always a nature that is not the construct of human culture and technology but is the primary condition and context of any cultural intervention and manipulation in the first place.

This applies equally to the larger-scale forms of human interaction with the environment, where there is always a distinction to be drawn between the powers and processes which are the essential precondition of all agricultural or horticultural practice, on the one hand, and the humanly modified landscape and its plant and animal life, on the other. For the most part (and one is presuming here that even the wilder reaches of the environment bear some traces, however minimal, of their human modification), it is 'nature' in this second sense which is the more directly experienced, and the object of our emotional and aesthetic responses. It is this 'nature', whether in the form of the panoramic landscape or the detail of flora and fauna, which we love as a source of beauty or solace, and whose 'loss' or 'destruction' is lamented. It is also, of course, nature under this aspect for which human beings must assume responsibility and exercise ecological choice. Nature conceived as fundamental powers and processes will set some limits on what we can do, or try to do, and it will have some say in shaping the outcome. But it is human policy makers who have to decide in what ways, and with what likely social and ecological consequences, they will harness these powers and work within their limits.

THE GARDEN
ANDREW MARVELL

For Marvell, as for many other poets of the
garden, the space it provides is that of an
actual retreat, which is also conceived more
metaphorically as providing a respite from
civil strife, social ambition and the 'incessant
labours' of life. This is shown in the opening
stanzas from 'The Garden' below.

How vainly men themselves amaze
To win the Palm, the Oke, or Bayes;
And their uncessant Labours see
Crown'd from some single Herb or Tree,
Whose short and narrow verged shade
Does prudently their Toyles upbraid;
While all Flow'rs and all Trees do close
To weave the Garlands of repose.

Fair quiet, have I found thee here,
And Innocence thy Sister dear!
Mistaken long, I sought you then
In busie Companies of Men.
Your sacred Plants, if here below,
Only among the Plants will grow:
Society is all but rude
To this delicious Solitude.

THE GARDEN

No place is more obviously a point of intersection of the natural
and the cultural, of botanical process, on the one hand, and human
management, on the other, than the garden. In this respect, the
National Botanic Garden of Wales provides an important reminder
and illustration of the difference between what is naturally
determined and what is humanly created. The garden also
symbolises the importance today of countering that type of
'wilderness' aesthetic which sees nature as surviving only in those

ABOVE Melanzana fructu
pallido: *an illustration*
of the aubergine plant
from the 'Hortus
Eystettensis' of Basil Besler
(1561–1629).

At the same time, in being both beautiful and bountiful, the botanic garden is a place where our instrumental need for nature as a set of resources is reconciled with our dependency upon it as a source of consolation and aesthetic pleasure. Some may deny that we do have a need for nature in this latter sense, and it is certainly true that this manifestation differs in important respects from those of, say, hunger or the need for protection from the elements. The needs for food and shelter will continue to be experienced even in the absence of gratification, and their satisfaction is essential to physical survival. If, on the other hand, we are deprived of the sensory delights of nature we do not die, and the experienced need for these may even wither or dry up altogether in the very lack of their provision. But the fact that those deprived of access to the sights and sounds of nature do not consciously feel a loss does not mean they have not sustained one.

We cannot doubt the appeal of the garden and its capacity to satisfy human needs. The enduring popularity of gardening testifies to this. So, too, does the plethora of garden imagery and symbolism that is found in human culture. Gardens have persisted since earliest times, and are a common feature of cultures that are in many other respects very diverse. There are few mythologies that do not contain their Arcadian or Edenic imagery, and few literatures that do not celebrate what Andrew Marvell refers to as the 'delicious solitude' and 'wondrous life' to be had in the garden.

No doubt the National Botanic Garden of Wales will also figure in some sense as a place of retreat from the rigours of work and the larger and uglier context of human interactions with nature. But it is to be hoped that as it does so, it also provides a site for reflecting on these contrasts, why they came to be there in the first place, and whether we should not now begin to reverse some of the processes that have made them so dramatic. Whereas in the past – as John Prest point outs in his contribution to this book – the great metropolitan botanic gardens in Britain, as elsewhere in Europe, have been instruments of imperialism, tied into exploitation of the colonised peoples and resources, the National Botanic Garden of Wales could signal the arrival of a new – more socially sensitive and ecologically responsible – phase in the history of the European botanic garden.

ABOVE Solanum pomiferum, *also from the 'Hortus Eystettensis' of Basil Besler.*

parts to which humanity has yet to reach. The idea that nature is respected or conserved only when it is protected from us, and that we humans get 'back to nature' only when we get back to the 'wild' is itself more of an escapist reaction to current ecological bad practice, than a remedy for it. The National Botanic Garden of Wales, in contrast, has no pretensions to be wilderness, but it is designed nonetheless with conservation in mind. It is ecologically self-sustaining; and it is dedicated to the nurturing and preservation of natural species.

CONSERVATION: OUT OF THE WILDERNESS

John O'Neill & Alan Holland

Why a new botanic garden now? Throughout their history botanic gardens have been responses to different concerns and interests. Some grew out of the 'physick gardens' attached to medical schools in European universities. Others served as living encyclopaedias and as scientific research centres. Botanic gardens have taken on symbolic roles – as attempts to re-create Eden and as colonial emblems of the power of empire. They have also been the instruments of real power – the royal gardens of Kew were transformed into a storehouse for the British Empire, and were a conduit through which commercial plants were transported across the globe.

So why a new garden now? The question is particularly poignant given the threats to a number of university botanic gardens, now perceived to have less relevance to biological teaching and research with the shift from whole plant biology to chemical, molecular and genetic studies. One important answer is that the botanic garden can help us to respond to the current environmental crisis. Environmental concerns around sustainability and the preservation

LEFT *A view in Kew Gardens of the Alhambra (c. 1798) by F J Manskirch — an illustration of the power of empire.*

OPPOSITE *Hunting in Yosemite (1890) by Thomas Hill — the image of wilderness.*

163

RIGHT *A mediterranean habitat in south-eastern Australia — human or natural territory?*

of biodiversity have been central to the founding vision of the National Botanic Garden of Wales. But what is the environmental crisis that we are taken to be facing? What are the concerns that the Garden is expressing? And what responses can it offer?

THE 'WILDERNESS' PROBLEM

For many environmentalists, especially those whose views are said to be 'deep green', the very idea that a garden could play any such role is likely to look implausible from the start. Environmentalism, especially as it has developed in the new world contexts of the USA and Australia, centres on a defence of 'wilderness', and of 'nature' understood as that which is free of human presence. Our environmental crisis is presented as involving 'the end of nature', where this is understood as the disappearance of a world unaffected by human activity.

If that is the crisis to which modern environmental concerns are a response, what role could a garden play? The garden is eminently an artificial and cultural entity, the product of human design and purpose. The mediterranean habitats that have been created in the Great Glasshouse, while native to the Mediterranean, are here more a witness to human ingenuity. The problem is neatly captured in this text from the National Botanic Garden's web-page:

> 'The fine landscaped gardens and parkland of now ruined Middleton Hall, lost for more than a century in a wilderness of scrub and marshland, are being reclaimed in one of the most ambitious environmental projects ever undertaken in Wales.'

For those who see the environmental crisis as involving the end of nature, to take 'a wilderness of scrub and marshland' and reclaim it as a garden is an act of environmental destruction, not an act of environmental restoration. What response might be made on behalf of the gardener?

If there is a problem here it is not just one that applies to the conservation efforts of botanic gardens. In Europe, there is little, if any, wilderness. The central conservation issues concern specific

environments which, typically, have a history of human use associated with a specific habitat. Conservation problems have arisen from abrupt changes in the use of the land: losses of meadowland herbs as a result of nitrogen applications and other intensive farming techniques, radical shifts in patterns of grazing, or the disappearance of hedgerows and copses to make way for efficient use of new machinery. The problems result from changing patterns of human use of a particular place, and not from intervention in a wilderness from which humans were previously absent. Given that the concept of wilderness is a central evaluative concept in 'deep green' evaluation, the very fact that European landscapes embody such a deal of human history entails that they constitute an environment that has little value.

Now this appraisal is not merely counter-intuitive, but it also relies on a fundamentally colonial image of new-world wilderness: an image of unspoilt pristine terrain dramatically different from the domesticated environments of Europe. 'Wilderness' too has had its role in the history of empire. Calling land wilderness was

THE OLIVE GROVE

Under glass, white cliffs over a ravine,

growing with carob, almond, pomegranate, palm,

an olive grove, two-hundred-and-fifty-year-old trees

from the arid mountains above Almuñecar.

They came veiled, bowed under mantillas

of horticultural fleece, against rain-loaded

earth-scented westerlies off the Atlantic.

Gillian Clarke

WILDERNESS — AN AMERICAN EXAMPLE

The wilderness question is nicely illustrated by the history of the management of one of the great symbols of American wilderness, Yosemite National Park. The influential Leopold report of 1963 *Wildlife Management in the National Parks* refers to 'the grass parkland, in springtime carpeted with wildflowers' encountered by the forty-niners who poured into the Sierra Nevada and California. The 'parkland' was the result of the pastoral practices of the indigenous people, who had used fire to promote pastures for game and black oak for acorn production.

After the Ahwahneechee Indians were driven from their homeland in 1851, 'Indian style' burning techniques were discontinued and fire suppression controls introduced. The consequence

BELOW *Yosemite National Park — the archetype of wilderness.*

was the decline in meadowlands under increasing areas of bush. When the Totuya, the granddaughter of chief Tenaya and sole survivor of the evicted Indians, returned in 1929, she remarked on the landscape she found, 'too dirty; too much bushy'. Following the Leopold report, environmental management employed both cutting and burning to 'restore' Yosemite to its 'primitive' state.

part of its designation as *terra nullius* — unowned land. This categorisation undermined the claims of indigenous peoples to the land and concealed the fact that those peoples had already shaped the landscape. The settlers were able to present the land as a pristine Eden that had awaited them. The wilderness model fails to acknowledge the fact that the 'wilderness' of the new world was not wilderness but home for its native inhabitants, with particular landscapes, flora and fauna that had cultural significance to the local populations. Moreover, it has had damaging and far-reaching consequences for environmental management. The treatment of nature as a primitive wilderness has led to a failure to appreciate the ecological impact of indigenous land management practices and a failure to understand that, to keep it in its 'pristine' condition, the 'natural' landscapes need to be managed in ways that reproduce the effects of older patterns of land use.

WILDERNESS AND GARDENING

Critics of environmental management sometimes make disparaging comparisons with gardening. Environmental management, it is said, is nothing but glorified gardening. How much difference is there between cutting back on 'the wilderness of scrub and marshland' to reclaim a garden, and cutting back scrub to reclaim a heathland or limestone pavement, or to reclaim Yosemite back to its 'primitive' state? Or between raising trees to restore some avenue and creating nurseries to re-establish forests and woodlands lost to grazing? Where does gardening finish and environmental management begin?

Perhaps it is possible to turn the point back on the wilderness conception of environmental value. When it is said that environmental management is just glorified gardening, we could re-interpret this as praise, rather than as criticism. Indeed, we could interpret the National Botanic Garden's concern with conservation as a response to current environmental problems, but there is a case for reading the situation in the opposite direction: current attempts to protect particular habitats and landscapes could be understood as moments in the history of gardening — as belonging to that lineage of wilderness gardening that goes back to the eighteenth century. As David Littlewood has suggested in *Between Nature and Culture: the Place of the Garden in Narrative Approaches to*

Environmental Value, our environmental concerns might be re-expressed as raising the question of how we should now garden the world we find ourselves in.

But there are difficulties, too, with this reversed reading. While the wilderness model of our environmental problems is flawed, so also is one that treats environmental concerns entirely in the language of gardens, however suggestive this might be. If environmental protection itself is just glorified gardening, one might wonder what we are conserving for. Rejecting the wilderness conception of conservation as specious will not help — the question remains still more starkly. Why garden in this way rather than that? Why conserve agricultural landscapes based on sheep farming with their particular habitats for flora and fauna, for example, rather than allow others to take their place? What are we conserving for?

SUSTAINABILITY AND BIODIVERSITY

Answers to the above questions, both in the environmental literature and in public policy statements, tend to be framed in the language of 'biodiversity' and 'sustainability'. Conservation is presented as a response to threats to losses in biodiversity: the loss of particular habitats, such as those mediterranean habitats with which the Great Glasshouse is particularly connected; the loss of particular species, say of Welsh ferns and bryophytes; and the loss of genetic diversity. Correspondingly, the goal of conservation is presented as that of 'sustaining' some stock of natural assets, sometimes described as 'natural capital'.

The sustaining of biodiversity is thought of as central to such a project. Given a list of valued items — habitat types, woodlands, heathlands, lowland grasslands, peatlands and species assemblages — we maintain our natural capital if, for any loss of these, we can recreate another with the same assemblages. However, this approach just begs the question: sustainability of what, for whom, for how long, and why? Merely keeping something going is not in itself of value. Nor do we necessarily think everything we value should be 'sustained', if by that we mean 'preserved in some particular state'. There are things we value in part because they are ephemeral: the rainbow, the shaft of sunlight, the evening with friends, different stages in the growth of our children. None of these should we want

ABOVE *Spore production by the male fern — a stock of natural assets?*

RIGHT *The interplay of human and natural histories: maidenhair spleenwort on an old wall.*

to preserve or conserve. While we may regret their passing, the considered answer to the question 'wouldn't it be great if it was like this forever?' would be 'no'. Likewise with particular conservation goals. Appeals to biodiversity as such don't fill the gap here. If one examines a palynologist's history of the pollen distribution on a site, one of the striking things to emerge is the degree to which species assemblages and habitats have changed over the centuries. It is not always clear what habitats and species assemblages we should now be trying to sustain into the future and why.

HISTORY AND PROCESS

Much current conservation thinking focuses on particular end states rather than on processes of change. In deliberation about environmental value, process and history matter. We value forests, lakes, mountains, wetlands and other habitats specifically for the history they embody. Geological features have histories with no human component, while landscapes often involve the interplay of human use and natural processes. Most current nature conservation problems are concerned with flora and fauna in sites

that have been shaped by a particular history of human pastoral and agricultural activity, rather than with sites that existed prior to human intervention. And the past is evident not only in the flora and fauna, but also in the embodiments of the work of previous human generations that form part of the landscape: stone walls, terraces, old irrigation systems and so on.

At the local level, the past matters, too, in the value that we put upon place. The value of specific locations is often a consequence of the way that the life of a community is embodied within them. This in turn contributes in large measure to their distinctiveness. Historical ties of community have a material dimension in both human and natural landscapes within which a community dwells. The natural world, landscapes humanised by pastoral and agricultural environments, and the built environment all take their value from the specific histories they contain. We enter worlds that are rich with past histories, the narratives of lives and communities from which our own lives take significance.

From this perspective, the question we should be asking is how to continue that history – what would make the most appropriate trajectory from what has gone before? As Alan Holland and Kate Rawles put it in their report to The Countryside Council for Wales *The Ethics of Conservation*:

> 'conservation is. . . about preserving the future as a realisation of the potential of the past. . . [it] is about negotiating the transition from past to future in such a way as to secure the transfer of maximum significance'.

Since conservation is about the negotiation of a narrative order between past and future, it is not simply about 'preserving the past'. Indeed, once the significance of the role of process and narrative is understood, we can perceive more clearly what is wrong with that preservationist approach. One major problem with the heritage industry and nature conservation policy is the way it often attempts to freeze historical development. A place then ceases to have a continuing story to tell. The object becomes a mere spectacle, a museum piece, taken outside of any common history.

If we consider processes rather than end states, some common ground between 'wilderness' and 'garden' approaches to

motion' (see pages 172–181) take account of change and propose attitudes to gardening that nurture the results of the unintended processes of nature. The organic gardening movement has also done much to change attitudes and foster sensitivity to natural processes. Such gardening does indeed exist in the new Botanical Garden – witness the lichens and fungi which flourish in the park at Middleton Hall and which will remain an important part of the botanical scenery of the new Garden.

RELATIONS

The lichens, the fungi, and the weeds display complex responses to their environments, yet the Great Glasshouse and many other components of the Garden remain expressions of human ingenuity. This is a cultural and artificial project and none the worse for that. What part, then, can such clearly cultural and artificial projects play in responding to environmental concerns? What is the role of these elements in the new Garden? We should not expect a simple answer to that question. Our environmental concerns reflect the complexity of our relations to our environments. The Garden as a response to those concerns needs to be similarly complex.

Consider our different relationships to environments. Environments, good and bad, and the objects they contain, matter to us in at least three important ways:

- We live from them – they are the means to our existence.
- We live in them – they are our homes and familiar places in which everyday life takes place and draws its meaning, and in which personal and social histories are embodied.
- We live with them – our lives take place against the backdrop of a natural world that existed before us and will continue to exist beyond the life of the last human, a world that we enter and for which awe and wonder are responses.

These different relations to the world all bring with them different sources of environmental concern, appreciation and sorrow. Through its scientific and educational programmes and its interpretative and cultural activities, the Garden is in a position to explore the complexities of human relations to the environment. It can contribute not only to knowledge relevant to immediate practical problems, for example in agriculture, but also to our understanding of the place that plants have in the lives and

ABOVE *Lichens on oak roots – natural processes independent of human intervention.*

conservation begins to emerge. Intentional human activities like the design of garden beds take place in the context of unintentional natural processes that proceed regardless of human intentions and indeed which often thwart them. Habitats may be the result of particular patterns of human activity, but were not the aim of those activities: skylarks and poppies, after all, were the unintended beneficiaries of farming practices, not their direct purpose. What is often valued in particular environments is the fortuitous interplay of human and natural histories. And too often environmental management rules out the unexpected and spontaneous.

Environmental management should not be modelled on the management plans of human industry. It needs to be responsive to processes that occur independently of human intentions. Certain traditions of gardening, where the spontaneous processes of the natural world are valued and steered, may have more to teach us about wider environmental management than we have hitherto thought. Gilles Clément's planetary gardens and his 'gardens in culture of people. And it can educate human sensitivity to the biological world that surrounds us, developing people's capacity to see and appreciate the commonplace as well as the charms of the distant exotic.

Finally, we should not forget that the Garden is also a space for reflection. Western philosophical reflection began in gardens, and among the first botanical gardens was that of Aristotle, with Theophrastus as curator. Gardens have remained places of contemplation. Much of that reflection will be, as it was for Aristotle, quite properly scientific and will carry forward his time-honoured concern with taxonomy. However, we also need to reflect on science itself. Public trust in the institutions of science,

and scientific spokespersons, has fallen in recent years. In particular, where science is a motor of technological change it is seen as itself a source of risk and uncertainty rather than a response to them. Nowhere is this more pressing than in the area of genetic engineering, and Middleton's genetic garden offers the opportunity of placing scientific reflection within an ethical and political context. Wider cultural reflection on the history of the relations of humans to plants is also properly at the heart of the Garden's programme. Those reflections are not just an end in themselves, but serve the role of environmental education in the wide sense of equipping citizens for the tasks of deliberating and negotiating a path towards a meaningful future with nature.

LEFT *Outside the Walled Garden at Middleton — a place for reflection.*

A BOTANIC GARDEN FOR THE PLANET

 Gilles Clément (*translated by Andrew Sclater*)

A botanic garden today is no longer only concerned with assembling collections and classifying species, its primary role is conservation.

At least two of the reasons for the disappearance of species from Earth have been identified. The first is competition among organisms (population dynamics), and the second is biological exclusion from the environment (pollution). Action taken against the first would interfere with the natural mechanism of evolution, whilst failure to take action against the second would amount to accepting biological suicide, life itself being at stake.

The worldwide intermingling of flora, fauna and human beings has gathered increasing momentum over the last one hundred years and is giving rise to a readjustment of equilibria among living systems. Long-standing balances are being disturbed and this, in turn, poses a threat to global biodiversity. If in some way this global intermingling is bringing with it a truly new landscape and forcing – as I believe – a new stage in the process of evolution, then we are justified in using all appropriate means to preserve those species which are endangered by its irrepressible mechanisms.

A botanic garden plays a part in both the classification and preservation of species. Yet one cannot imagine knowledge developing dynamically in an institution where the sole objectives were classification and protection of the natural world, as this would confine the garden to being simply a scientific project devoted to the naming, description and systematic classification of species.

A botanic garden is more than this – it is the colours, textures, shapes, scents and birdsong, and above all light and shade. It is the insects and their predators, the fungi and lichens, the mosses and the earth, sand and water and, sometimes, fire and storm too. It is about life and the complex relationships among living beings that share every square metre of the Earth.

WHAT'S BECOME OF NATURAL HISTORY?

A garden is a matrix of relations in which the botanical elements provide only a fragmentary index of our knowledge of the whole. This remains the case even when scientists single out a particular plant as a good biological indicator of certain ecological conditions.

Advances in biology have led us to look at organisms at very high resolution. Sometimes this examination is of the cell, chromosome or gene – those infinitesimal particles which can belong to any living being. Plants have not escaped this reduction to the common denominator, which in turn drains them of their vitality and virtually reduces them to mathematical formulae.

Admittedly, the high level of detail at which we can now read biological processes does have the advantage of bringing to light the uniqueness of the mechanism of life. This is particularly the case in genetics, where we can be reduced to simple chemical formulae – a few acids and some bases on the DNA spiral. Conversely, it is from these simple formulae that we have developed, by a series of genetic modifications.

If we consider the animal-vegetable distinction – the clearest of all differences established by traditional classifications – we see that it is becoming increasingly blurred. It may even be fundamentally questionable. All this challenges the legitimacy of a garden established to be exclusively botanical. In a more general sense, it raises questions about the natural sciences. How should they be taught? Can there be a systematic and globalising way of teaching, or must we still make use of analytical and divisive techniques?

If a botanic garden were to define itself as a centre for conservation – and we have seen this issue to be an important one – what should it conserve? Should it emphasise biological species or biological systems, or both? Can we imagine a pedagogical system which functions by means of an index in which all the individual elements, in this case every single plant, relates back to the whole of the system to which it belongs?

For several decades, progress in the natural sciences has led to improvements in our understanding of behaviour, both of the characteristic behaviour of a species and of the behavioural relationship of that species to its environment. However, the study of relationships between species, that is 'ecology' in its strict scientific sense, is so complex that our current knowledge throws far less light upon the relationship of a species to its environment than upon its internal functions. The work of ethologists, ethnobotanists and behavioural scientists is out-performed by those biologists who tease apart and unravel the cellular microcosm of life.

Consequently, an immense field of investigation remains open to botany. An opportunity exists for botanists to recognise that the plant is an interdependent part of a complex system, that naming should be based on behavioural identity rather than on the traditional criteria of reproductive organs or chemical constituents. The planting and layout of modern botanic gardens should be designed appropriately to reflect these concerns.

THE GARDEN AS PLANETARY INDEX

Whether gorse (*Ulex europaeus*) belongs to the super-family Leguminosae or to the Fabaceae is a minor, albeit necessary,

issue. Apart from the odd skirmish between specialists, the matter has been settled. More important is the fact that this very same gorse, while 'behaving itself properly' in the hedges of Brittany, is also invading South Island in New Zealand and even making unexpected appearances at 2000 metres above sea level in La Réunion in the Pacific Ocean. In today's botanic garden, both plant and planet should be included in the same perspective. Each species must be seen in relation to its changing behaviour on Earth.

ABOVE *Pioneer species colonising the ground after fire at Sandy Bay, on the west flank of Table Mountain, South Africa.*

intermingling. By studying this phenomenon, we should be able to understand the global range and performance of a given species better, and to supplement data on its morphological and genetic diversity with new information on its behavioural diversity. In this respect, and regardless of its geographical position, a botanic garden has the opportunity to become a planetary index.

Such an index should not only include 'natural' data about species, but also data on the 'cultural relations' of species. Connections should be made to traditional and abiding relations between nature and cultures, rather than to the affirmation of a single culture's supremacy. By abdicating its separation of the world of plants from the rest of the living world, and by signing up to a global system of reference, botany could open up a new pathway towards a fuller understanding of the world.

THE INDIVIDUAL PLANT AT THE HEART OF THE LIVING WORLD

Any pathway to understanding the system in which we are evolving cannot confine itself to plants alone, although it must of necessity pass their way. The animal world cannot be studied effectively without constant reference to plants. Since the opposite is not quite true, some botanists such as Francis Hallé, Director of the Laboratory of Tropical Botany at Montpellier, believe plants to have a more secure future as part of this planet than all other types of organism.

The supremacy of plants is due to their unique technological advantage – the chlorophyll factory. This makes even the puniest of plants autotrophic, or in other words self-sufficient in energy terms. By comparison, animals, which are predators for the most part, seem archaic, clumsy and exceedingly dependent on their environment, consisting as it does mainly of plants.

However, animals compensate for this 'clumsiness' by being extremely mobile. An ability to move may be one of the defining characteristics of an animal, but plants seem to be entirely fixed to a given place. This apparently essential difference does not stand up to comparative analysis when we consider the conquest of earth by animals and plants. It is the plants which always win. The term 'pioneer species' relates to plants and can only be used for animals and humans in a metaphorical sense. Only plants are able to

We should be in a position to investigate behavioural differences within a single species. In some places gorse regenerates in equilibrium with different species, while in others its regeneration prevents anything else but gorse from growing. In the first case, a biodiverse landscape begins to develop into what will eventually be a forest. In the second, the landscape is fixed by the scrubby character of a single species. Most of the species that could be termed 'cosmopolitan' take part in the process of worldwide

RIGHT *Global intermingling – the South African* Cryophytum crystallinum *now grows on sandy shores in all mediterranean climate zones, as here at La Serena, in Chile.*

LEFT *These European mulleins (*Verbascum thapsus) *are a common sight in the Australian Snowy Mountains.*

establish themselves on bare land and survive *in situ* (unless one classifies certain primitive organisms such as bacteria as animals!).

The means by which plants spread themselves are well known. Every agent of dispersal is made use of: winds, sea currents, animal fur, car and aeroplane tyres, the soles of our shoes, and so on. Plants usually travel in the form of seeds, produced by fertilisation, and specially structured to resist the wear and tear of a lengthy journey and to preserve the life which they contain. What animal embryo could survive outside the womb? With the principal exception of certain insects, animals cannot survive without a constant supply of fuel to meet their energy needs. By contrast with the autotrophic plants, animals are definitively subjugated to their environment: they have to obtain food.

The global intermingling of flora clearly demonstrates this potential of plants for conquest and testifies to their mobility. The apparent immobility of a plant in its growing phase does not prevent it from moving in time and space. In fact, some species can move to a greater extent during their growing phase than during their reproductive phase. This applies chiefly to herbaceous perennials which develop and spread progressively across relatively modest areas, by various means such as stolons, offsets, and so on. However, sexual reproduction remains the dominant mechanism for mobility in most plants, including the great majority of trees, and certain species rely on this method entirely, as the parent plants die after producing their seeds.

SPREADING THE SEED

In temperate climates, the majority of plants which die after producing seeds are the so-called annuals and biennials. Collectively, according to Raunkiaer's biological spectrum, they may be categorised as therophytes on the basis of their behaviour, i.e. briefly developing a visible growing structure, at an appropriate moment during a longer life cycle. Desert plants often lie hidden in the sands for up to 20 years. When they at last germinate, stems and leaves are rapidly produced and they sometimes flower within a mere two weeks. Such plants are therophytes, and cornfield flowers (poppies, cornflowers and corncockles) behave in a similar way, as do all other short life-cycle plants.

THEROPHYTES

Therophytes, such as poppies, cornflowers and corncockles, are plants which tend to exist far longer as seeds than as stem, leaf and flower. *Eschscholzia* **and** *Cosmos* **are therophytes from California and Mexico respectively. They can be found in countries as far from their 'home' as Tasmania and Madagascar; the distances they are able to travel in their protective seed case testify to their performance as survivors and conquerors.**

ABOVE *Cornflowers (*Centaurea cyanus) *are typical therophytes. They used to grow in cornfields, completing their life cycle quicker than the corn, until weedkillers drove them out.*

Strangely enough, this aspect of plant behaviour is rarely demonstrated in botanic gardens. While it may be hard to do much in design terms with seeds on their own, leaving out these fundamental components of life amounts to blanking out the future: all of the future is contained either in seeds or in eggs.

It may be worth using this perspective to consider the oldest botanical families, like the Ranunculaceae and the Magnoliaceae whose heavy seeds fall directly below the plant and germinate at very low frequency, in comparison with more recent products of evolution like members of the Gramineae and Asteraceae whose light seeds fly in the wind by virtue of their pappi or other aerodynamic devices and germinate at high frequency. The small number of progeny and restricted geographical range of the former provide clear evidence that the future lies with the latter. It is also clear that the vegetation of our landscapes is destined to be marked permanently by increases in certain species at the expense of others. This leads us to conclude that a botanic garden's conservation role should feature the preservation of species that are naturally destined to give up their place to more successful conquerors. Yet it would not be right to disregard the vagabond species that are attacking our planet, for the good reason that they are actively determining our future. It is hardly surprising that a so-called weed from South America, *Chromolaena odorata*, is spreading all over the tropical world, particularly in Africa, because its seeds germinate very well, are efficiently dispersed by wind and are highly resistant to fire. It has very recently been shown that this invasive member of the Asteraceae family is helping forest to colonise the African savannah. Clearly, by virtue of a synergy between indigenous and exotic species, local landscapes can be profoundly transformed and, in this case, for the better. The extent of such change is independent of the physical size of the species in question: a tiny plant can alter the landscape and change human life.

WHAT IS MEANT BY INDIGENOUS FLORA?

When one considers botany and its systems of ordering and classification, one question remains more and more difficult to answer: how do we define the indigenous flora? Can we still talk of particular plants being indigenous to particular areas if all

ABOVE *The changing landscape at Middleton.*

From the point of view of performance and supremacy on earth, therophytes are better adapted than all other plants to survive climate change, natural disaster, wars and so on. Their system of dormancy, or suspended animation in a protective seed case, together with their fitness for travelling, provide the wherewithal for survival in time. Eschscholzias and cosmos are therophytes from California and Mexico respectively, and are distributed over vast areas of Tasmania and Madagascar. Unsurprisingly, most of the plants that have been designated 'problem weeds' are therophytes.

systems which seem to be located within a specific region are evolving, changing, being enriched by 'exotic' flora and fauna, and are producing new forms and new landscapes? Indigenous at what point in time? In the early Quaternary or today? Europe's history of glaciations and subsequent thaws has produced both polar and tropical landscapes, and the species that were indigenous, or native, to any region of these past landscapes were very different from those we find there today.

Is it anachronistic for centres of conservation such as the efficient botanic gardens of Kirstenbosch in Cape Town, or those at Canberra, New South Wales, only to concern themselves with the flora of South Africa or Australia? These centres are very elaborate, both scientifically and aesthetically, and their prime purpose is to display indigenous diversity to the end of saving it more effectively. But there appears to be no subsidiary aim behind their magnificent work, other than the potential for commercialising material supposed to be lying somewhere in the gene pool. Meanwhile, before our very eyes, all over the world there are processes taking place on a vast scale which could conceivably be mustered to economic advantage. The small *Acacia cyclops* is grown at the Canberra Botanic Garden although nothing is said of its usefulness in stabilising Moroccan sand dunes, nor of

ABOVE *Californian tree lupins, mauve cinerarias from Madeira and a Moneterey pine far from home here at Palmerston North, New Zealand.*

LEFT *At Cape Town, Kirstenbosch botanists have re-created a flowering meadow, rich in* Gazania *and* Osteospermum, *from another South African region — Namaqualand.*

ROCK

The garden turns in space
under the summer planets,
Venus's lamp in the west,
and Mars, the red eye
of the last wolf.

*

In the subdivisions of geological time
Earth-story has two parts:
pre-Cambrian, Phanerozoic,
chaptered with eras,
paragraphed with epochs, ages, chrons,

sedimentary time
laid down and shaped
with the patience of stone,
silt on silt, microbe, algae,
trilobite, brachiopod,

first jellyfish, first worm,
leaf-mould, bone on bone.
Then the long upheavals
as continents slide, like folding
plates of a baby's skull.

Gillian Clarke

its invasion of the Cape fynbos and the ecological disruption which that is causing. In other words, nothing is done to connect indigenous Australian flora with its counterparts elsewhere in the world. This is probably because the notion of the indigenous in the natural sciences is being assimilated progressively into a more general notion of heritage, and each country, in trying to protect its own heritage, believes that the indigenous should remain and be protected in its homeland. In biological terms, this makes no sense at all. Nature, perpetually evolving, by its changeability defies heritage status. Arguably, the phrase 'natural heritage' may be applied to a landscape but it is most definitely not applicable to living organisms.

ABOVE *Rice growing in Bali is closely linked to the world view of the Balinese – descriptions of plants should record their significance to people.*

THE PLANETARY GARDEN TODAY

A botanic garden has immense potential to present knowledge via the form of living organisms at their most moving – when they are complete, colourful, fragile and alive. This represents a real advantage over the biology laboratory in which life appears as abstracted forms to which it is impossible to put a face.

What is more, a botanic garden reveals the diversity of its plants and, beyond formal taxonomic diversity, it can or should demonstrate their behavioural diversity too. There is nothing banal about such diversity: through their achievements and their great ability to adapt, plants have a better chance of surviving in the long term than any other organism. Similarly, we must take

care not to overlook even the smallest of grasses: the future may depend upon it.

It seems clear that a botanic garden presents a globalising way of seeing the world, even when this is not deliberately intended. The relationships among plants and animals, and in particular the relations between humans and plants, ask us to view the world in this way. Let us remember that most of the cultivated plants on earth are not botanically 'original' but have been 'improved' by us, nor have we cultivated them only in the countries from which they originated. Regardless of whether a botanic garden devotes itself to an allegedly indigenous flora, or takes account of a more cosmopolitan dimension, the network established by planetary intermingling has become inevitable. The task now is to establish how best to explain this phenomenon, and decide which teaching method should be used. Should we opt for one that elevates nature and regards it as sacred, or should we choose instead to see nature and humans in a symbiotic relationship and invent a humanist botanic garden?

ABOVE *Paddy fields in Bali, cut into the hillsides where 'indigenous' and 'exotic' species intermingle.*

LOOKING AHEAD —
THE GARDEN IN 2050

Charles Stirton

'Landscape creates nations, and nowhere is the truism truer than in Wales, Cymru, which is a bumpy squarish protrusion on the western flank of England. Almost everything about Wales has been decreed by its terrain; certainly if the countryside had been different the Welsh people as we know them would never have existed.'

Jan Morris

'The Welsh, Cornish and Manx are three Celtic peoples who live between the English and the Atlantic, and who subscribe in varying degrees to the over-arching notion of British identity without the sacrifice of their distinct self-perceptions as historic communities' (F Fernandez-Armesto, *The Guide to the Peoples of Europe*). Recently, Wales and two other Celtic Arc countries, Scotland and Northern Ireland, began moving towards varying degrees of autonomy. The end of this process is uncertain but whatever ensues will have profound long-term influences on the future of Great Britain and the British Isles. Gardens will not escape these influences.

Three years ago, I left Kew Gardens to take up the challenge of helping to build the National Botanic Garden of Wales. When I arrived in Wales I had little knowledge of the country, its culture and its history. I had come to build a national and international botanic garden. I was attracted by the opportunity provided by the far-sighted trustees who wished to try something innovative

OPPOSITE *Reflections of ancient olive trees on the concourse wall of the Great Glasshouse.*

without being too prescriptive. At that stage in 1996 the garden was called Middleton Botanic Garden. It was not yet a national institution in name. By changing its name to The National Botanic Garden of Wales the project had to consider a broader constituency and geographic representation, and take proper account of the essence of Welshness. All of this took place during a period of intense political transformation in Wales and the United Kingdom. The political influences included policy objectives for organisations to adopt a more environmental approach to design and operations. Our responses to the complex influences surrounding the genesis of the Garden culminated in 'The philosophy of the Garden' published on the Garden's website in 1999 (see jacket for details).

This celebratory book has provided me with an opportunity to look ahead at the Garden's future. I will do this in the spirit of Professor Wynn Jones who wrote that 'Our greatest challenge is for people to identify and strive for a "preferred future", not simply resign themselves to a probable future.' The preferred future I anticipate is a personal one, as the actual future will derive also from the contributions and ideas of the trustees, future visitors and a broad range of other stakeholders. It will too be influenced and modified by future political and economic developments in West Wales and throughout the country. For these reasons, I make some basic premises which may or may not come to pass and will describe the National Botanic Garden of Wales as I see it in 2050.

What sort of world will the Director of the Garden live in as he or she sits down to write the Annual Review in 2050? Will Wales be an independent country, still be part of the United Kingdom or part of Europia? Will the Garden continue to enjoy Royal support? Will the internet have delivered its phenomenal promise of the millennium? Will the impact of nanotechnology (miniaturised machines) and its incorporation into biological tissues be reality? Will China, Brazil, and India be superpowers? There are many imponderables. With answers to many such questions only guessed at I have prepared a draft Annual Review for 2050.

THE GARDEN IN 2050

'This year is our 50th Anniversary since the official opening of the Garden in 2000. As the first new botanic garden to be established in the 3rd Millennium the Garden carried the hopes of many for a new way in public gardens. How have we fared over these last 50 years?

The National Botanic Garden of Wales now comprises 4 regional Gardens, with its flagship garden in Llanarthne, Carmarthenshire. Over 1 million visitors are attracted annually to the innovative gardens with their stunning horticultural displays and exhibits. The Garden employs 246 staff living in 16 countries and runs 3 virtual overseas offices and 2 joint overseas technology transfer centres.

A highlight of the horticultural calendar in Wales is the Garden's annual International Flower Festival held in Cardiff Castle and the Millennium Stadium. It attracts plant lovers from all around the world. Visitors from Europe and abroad are attracted by the superb transport infrastructure. This ranges from the refurbished international airport with direct links to major destinations, the green and artistic SUSTRANS cycle networks that criss-cross Wales, the restored light railways and small bus networks and the refurbished and extended canal transport system. There has been a major resurgence of interest in gardens as new developments in holo- and virtual-TV have made most theme parks of the early 2000s redundant. Semi-natural areas, parks and gardens are now very fashionable places as people increasingly need to connect to the few remaining belts of nature in the United Kingdom.

Wales is now one of the major garden destinations in Europe for tourists. It comprises four major tours: the Tywi Valley Gardens Tour, the Celtic Garden Circle (Wales and Ireland), the Celtic Arc Heritage Tour and the Premier Gardens of Wales Tour. Carmarthenshire is known as the Garden County of Wales and is the centre of a thriving horticultural industry, supported by the horticultural training facility and business incubator at Middleton Hall as well as the many local specialist nurseries and small manufacturers of horticultural products. These projects were successfully established under the Objective 1 regional assistance programme of the old European Union.

The arts continue to flourish at the Garden and the biennial International Symposium "Science meets the Arts" has reached its 25th year. This year's conference will be held live across 9 countries and the theme will be "Nanoscience: Beautiful but is it dangerous?"

The Great Glasshouse has been refurbished. The key new attraction is "Virtual Cell" – a journey through a living cell in any of the 3500 species growing in the Glasshouse. Most of the original mediterranean plants have been moved outside the main building, as the winters have become milder from global warming.

Work has begun on the new Invasive Species Centre, which will focus on the increased threat being posed to British wildlife by new water weeds and grassland invaders. The Garden's weed research continues in partnership with CAB International and various universities and county councils. Although Japanese knotweed has been eradicated from the United Kingdom for over 30 years through the safe introduction of a rust fungus and a stem borer from Japan, there are now some intractable invasive weeds that need attention.

The final results of the 50-year global warming monitoring experiment begun in 2000 on the estate of Middleton Hall will be published this year and will confirm that the predictions made in 2010 were largely correct. A regular 5-year monitoring programme of the plants and animals of the estate has been carried out since 2000 . Only 5 of the 18,000 plant species introduced to the Garden have proved invasive beyond the boundaries. In all cases their spread was detected and the plants eradicated. A public campaign continues across Wales against the sale and growing of these garden plants.

This month celebrates the 45th anniversary of Biodiagnostics Plc and Physicians of Myddfai Plc, the first two companies to graduate from Cambrian Ventures (the Garden's business incubator attached to the Science Centre). The three newest companies to graduate have been named Virtual Oomics (virtual genetic engineering), Nanosystematics Plc (rapid identification by in-cell nanochemistry), and Space Probes (automated planet life probes). The New Horizons Science Parks in West Carmarthen and Swansea are now leading centres of nanobiology in Europia.

The Plant Medicines Centre opens its doors this year with a new exhibit on the pharma-chemistry of complex traditional remedies. The exhibit describes the scientific breakthroughs that explain why so many traditional mixtures were so efficacious, and why it was possible for scientists to recreate complex mixtures of traditional herbal remedies. Today we can choose between using either plant extracts or synthesised medicines. The Garden has always, since its earliest exhibition on traditional Welsh medicines, striven to build bridges between traditional and mainstream medicine.

The autumn and spring colours of the National Arboretum were spectacular last year, attracting many visitors, especially as two of the forest systems represented are now extinct in the wild. The Garden is beginning a co-operative restoration programme with the Republic of Cameroon to help restore the temperate forest on Mount Cameroon, which was almost completely destroyed by a volcanic eruption three years ago. The spiritual centres representative of each woodland analogue region, and built in the 2010s, have seen a sharp rise in popularity.

There has also been an increase in the number of people who are now walking the entire estate, especially since the organic farm has been converted into analogue temperate habitats and additional specialist horticultural features. The Garden's support for organic farming and horticulture was very successful for 20 years, playing a key role in establishing organic farming and horticulture on sound economic and environmental principles. But with new safe advances in plant breeding and the great success of Welsh agriculture, it was felt that the Garden should convert the area to global habitats now under greater threat. Wisely, however, the 1920s Carmarthenshire working farm next to the restored Tudor

Gardens of the original Middleton Hall (pre-1790) were retained and refurbished. They continue to be a major attraction, surpassed only by the Double Walled Garden, with its new fountain and water features. The apple and pear orchards fruited heavily this year making the apple and pear festivals the best in a decade. The Honey Centre continues to attract visitors who come to see the active hives, still resistant to Dance Virus, which has damaged most of the remaining colonies in western Europia.

The Endowment Fund continues to grow and has enabled the Garden to become financially independent for the second time in its history. The recent legacy of 12 million euros from an anonymous donor will enable us to refurbish the Insect Centre in our East Regional Garden and extend the Mycodome, adding a new gallery on tropical fungi.

Friends of the Garden will be pleased to learn that additional seed packages from our successful Heritage Garden Seeds project will be available this year. This is largely due to the work of volunteers in our North Regional Garden.

As this is our 50th Anniversary, we will be celebrating through a retrospective look at the work and dreams of the pioneers who made our gardens possible and so enriched our lives. The theme of the events will be "Preferred Futures of the Founders". As a highlight we hope to receive on site some of the 1,200 international graduates of our many distance-learning courses.'

ABOVE *The annual glass cleaning requires a highly manoeuvrable platform, with a long reach.*

TAKING THE PLANET HOME

The approaching cars' white-gold moth-eyes

flare home at dusk. The cars touch down in silence,

beyond glass, on the runways of the M4.

Up and away from us, going our way,

red eyes of the wolf

from the last lost wilderness,

jewels of the rock cracked open for a fossil,

grains of mica in granite,

a handful of stars.

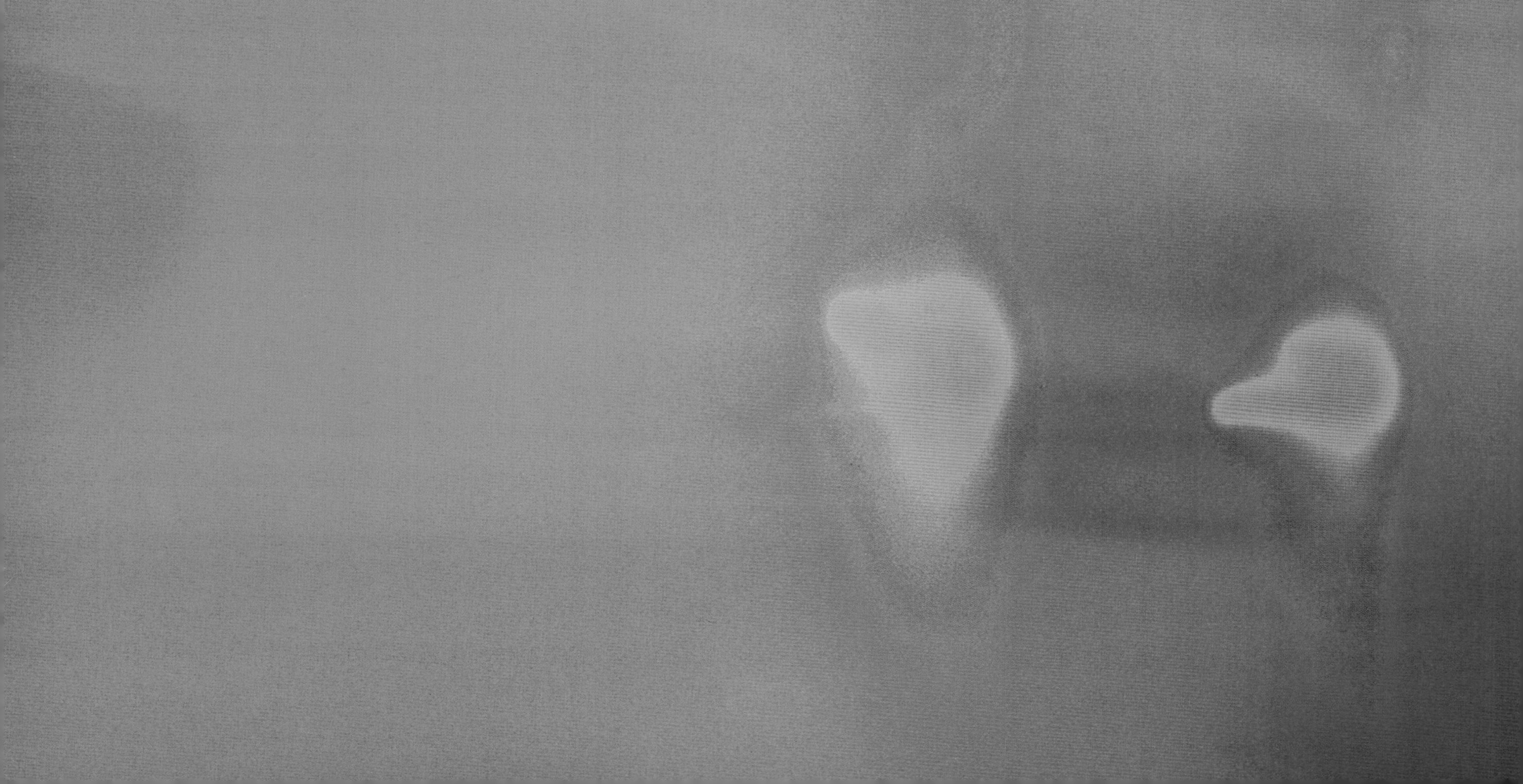

SUGGESTED READING

Andrew Sclater

Appleton, Jay *The Experience of Landscape* (revised edition), Wiley, 1996

Condry, William M. *The Natural History of Wales* (2nd edition), Bloomsbury, 1990

Jacques, David *Georgian Gardens: The Reign of Nature*, Batsford, 1983

Jellicoe, Geoffrey & Susan; Goode, Patrick & Lancaster, Michael *The Oxford Companion to Gardens*, Oxford University Press, 1986

Jones, Francis *Historic Carmarthenshire Homes and their Families*, Dyfed County Council, 1987

Lloyd, Thomas *The Lost Houses of Wales*, SAVE Britain's Heritage, 1986

Pope, Alexander 'Epistle to Lord Burlington' in *The Genius of the Place: The English Landscape Garden 1620–1820*, Dixon Hunt, J. & Willis, Peter (eds), MIT Press, 1988

Schama, Simon *Landscape and Memory*, HarperCollinsPublishers, 1995

Whittle, Elisabeth (for Cadw: Welsh Historic Monuments) *The Historic Gardens of Wales*, HMSO, 1992

John Prest

Arnold, D. *Imperial medicine and indigenous societies*, Manchester University Press, 1988

Carter, Harold B. *Sir Joseph Banks*, 1743-1820, British Museum, 1988

Crosby, Alfred W. *Ecological imperialism: the biological expansion of Europe, 900–1900*, Cambridge University Press, 1993

Desmond, Ray *Kew: the history of the Royal Botanic Gardens*, Harvill, 1995

Drayton, Richard *Nature's Government: Kew Gardens, Science, and Imperial Britain*, Yale University Press, forthcoming

Foust, Clifford M. *Rhubarb: the wondrous drug*, Princeton University Press, 1992

Grove, Richard H. *Green imperialism: colonial expansion, tropical island Edens and the origins of environmentalism, 1600–1860*, Cambridge University Press, 1995

Headrick, D.R. *The tentacles of progress: technology transfer in the age of imperialism*, Oxford University Press, 1988

Heniger, J. *Hendrik Adriaan van Reede tot Drakenstein (1636–1691) and Hortus Malabaricus: a contribution to the history of Dutch colonial botany*, A A Balkema, Rotterdam, 1986

McClellan, J.E. *Colonialism and science: Saint Domingue in the old regime*, Johns Hopkins University Press, 1992

McCracken, Donal P. *Gardens of empire: botanical institutions of the Victorian British empire*, Leicester University Press, 1997

Masefield, G.B. 'Crops and Livestock' in Rich, E.E. & Wilson, C.H. (eds), *The Cambridge Economic History of Europe, vol. 4, The economy of expanding Europe in the sixteenth and seventeenth centuries*, Cambridge University Press, 1967

Prest, John *The garden of Eden, the botanic garden and the re-creation of paradise*, Yale University Press, 1981

Ivor Stokes

Bean, W.J. *Trees and Shrubs Hardy in the British Isles*, John Murray, 1970

Beard, J.S. *Plant Life of Western Australia*, Kangaroo Press, 1990

Cowling, Richard & Richardson, Dave *Fynbos South Africa's Unique Floral Kingdom*, Fernwood Press, 1995

Dallman, Peter *Plant Life in the World's Mediterranean Climates*, Oxford University Press, 1998

Erickson, Rica *Flowers and Plants of Western Australia*, Reed, 1973

Kingsbury, Noel *The New Perennial Garden*, Frances Lincoln, 1996

Krüssman, G *Manual of Cultivated Conifers*, Batsford, 1985

Krüssman, G *Manual of Cultivated Broad-Leaved Trees and Shrubs*, Batsford, 1986

Jay Appleton

Borrow, George *Wild Wales. Its People, Language and Scenery*, John Murray, 1862

Dyer, John *Grongar Hill*, 1726

Gilpin, Revd. William *Observations on Several Parts of the Counties of Cambridge, Norfolk, Suffolk and Essex. Also on Several Parts of North Wales relative chiefly to Picturesque Beauty, in two tours, the former made in 1769, the latter in 1773*, Cadell & Davies, 1809

Howard, Peter *Landscapes: The Artists' Vision*, Routledge, 1991

Wordsworth, William *A Guide through the District of the Lakes in the North of England, with a Description of the Scenery, &c. for the Use of Tourists and Residents*, (Definitive 5th edition) Hudson & Nicholson, 1835

James Robertson

Condry, William M. *The Natural History of Wales*, Bloomsbury Books, 1993

Ellis, R.G. *Flowering Plants of Wales*, National Museum of Wales, 1983

Gerarde's *Herball*, 1683

Hoffman, David *Welsh Herbal Medicine*, Abercastle Publications, 1992

Mabey, Richard *Flora Britannica*, Sinclair-Stevenson, 1997

Quarrie, Joyce *Earth Summit '92: The United Nations Conference on Environment and Development; Rio de Janeiro*, Regency Press, 1992

Woods, Ray *Flora of Radnorshire*, National Museum of Wales, 1993

Peter Harper

Borer, Pat & Harris, Cindy *The Whole House Book*, CAT Publications, 1998 – a manual of environmental building and energy

Harper, Peter & Thorpe, Dave *Crazy Idealists!* CAT Publications, 1995 – a history of CAT

Harper, Peter; Light, Jeremy & Madsen, Chris *The Natural Garden Book*, Gaia Books, 1994

Henry Doubleday Research Association *Guidelines for Organic Gardening* (revised annually)

Hills, Lawrence D. *Fighting Like the Flowers*, Green Books, 1995 – a history of the HDRA

Owen, Jennifer *The Ecology of a Garden* Cambridge, 1991

Pears, P. & Steele, Judy (eds) *Organic Grounds Maintenance*, Organic Horticulture Association, 1998

The Soil Assocation *Organic Standards* (revised annually)

Whitelaw, Ken *ISO 14001 Environmental System Handbook*, Butterworth, 1997

Michael Rustin

Dawkins, Richard *The Selfish Gene*, Penguin, 1976

Dawkins, Richard *The Blind Watchmaker*, Penguin, 1990

Gould, Stephen Jay *Wonderful Life: the Burgess Shale and the Nature of History*, Penguin, 1989

Latour, Bruno *Science in Action*, Harvard University Press, 1987

Latour, Bruno & Woolgar, Steve *The Pasteurisation of France*, Sage, 1979

Williams, Raymond *The Country and the City*, Chatto and Windus, 1973

Williams, Raymond *Keywords*, Fontana, 1976

Kate Soper

Benton, Ted *Natural Relations*, Verso, 1993

Coates, Peter *Nature: Western Attitudes since Ancient Times*, Polity Press, 1998

Collingwood, R.C. *The Idea of Nature*, Oxford University Press, 1965

Evernden, Neil *The Social Creation of Nature*, Johns Hopkins University Press, 1992

Glacken, C.J. *Traces on the Rhodian Shore, Nature and Culture in Western Thought*,
    University of California Press, 1967

Haraway, Donna *Simians, Cyborgs and Women: the Reinvention of Nature*, London,
    Free Association and Routledge, 1991

Kemal, Salim & Gaskell, Ivan (eds) *Landscape, Natural Beauty and the Arts*,
    Cambridge University Press, 1993

Lovejoy, A.O. *The Great Chain of Being*, Harvard University Press, 1964

Macnaghten, Phil & Urry, John *Contested Natures*, Sage, 1998

Passmore, John *Man's Responsibility for Nature* (2nd edition), Duckworth, 1980

Soper, Kate *What is Nature: Culture, Politics and the Non-Human*, Blackwell, 1995

Thomas, Keith *Man and the Natural World*, Allen Lane, 1983

Wilson, Alexander *The Culture of Nature*, Oxford, 1991

John O'Neill & Alan Holland

Baird, J. Callicott & Nelson, M. *The Great Wilderness Debate*, University of Georgia Press, 1998

Cronon, W. *Uncommon Ground: Toward Reinventing Nature*, W.W. Norton, 1995

Foster, J. (ed) *Valuing Nature*, Routledge, 1997

Grove, R. *Green Imperialism: Colonial Expansion, Tropical Island Edens and
    the Origins of Environmentalism 1600–1860*, Cambridge University Press, 1995

Jamieson, D. (ed) *Blackwell Companion to Environmental Philosophy*, Blackwell, 1999

Littlewood, D. *Between Nature and Culture: the Place of the Garden in Narrative Approaches to
    Environmental Value*, Thingmount series, British Association of Nature
    Conservationists/Lancaster University, 2000

MacKenzie, J. *The Empire of Nature: Hunting, Conservation and British Imperialism*,
    Manchester University Press, 1988

O'Neill, J. *Ecology, Policy and Politics: Human Well-Being and the Natural World*, Routledge, 1993.

Rolston III, H. *Environmental Ethics*, Temple University Press, 1988

Gilles Clément

Cronk, C.B. & Fuller, J.L. *Plant Studies I*, Chapman & Hall, 1975

Good, R. *The Geography of the Flowering plants*, Longman, 1974

Groves, R.H. & Di Castri, F. *Biogeography of Mediterranean invasions*, Cambridge University Press, 1991

Gunn, Dr. & Dennis, J.V. *World guide to tropical drift seeds and fruits*, Quadrangle, 1976

Hallé, F. *Un Pays sans Hiver*, Seuil, 1993

Hallé, F. *Éloge de la Plante*, Seuil, 1999

Laborit, H. *Biologie et Structure*, Gallimard Folio Essai, 1968

Les Cahiers du Conservatoire du Littoral No 2 *Forêt Méditerranéenne: Vivre avec le Feu?*, 1993

Ozenda, P. *Les Végétaux dans la Biosphère*, Doin, 1982

Charles Stirton

Fernandez-Armesto, F. *The Guide to the Peoples of Europe*, Times Books, 1994

PLANT INDEX

INDEX